ACCESS TO SHAKESPEARE

The Tragedy of
Macbeth

A Facing-pages Translation into Contemporary English

Edited by
Jonnie Patricia Mobley, Ph.D.
Drama Department
Cuesta College
San Luis Obispo, California

Lorenz Educational Publishers
P.O. Box 711030, Los Angeles, CA 90071-9625

Cover border taken from the First Folio (1623)

Cover design by Tamada Brown Design, Chicago

Interior design and typesetting by David Corona Design, Dubuque

Published by Lorenz Educational Publishers. © 1995 by Lorenz Educational Publishers, PO Box 711030, Los Angeles, California 90071-9625. All rights reserved. No part of this book may be reproduced, stored in a retrieval system, or transmitted in any form or by any means without the prior permission of Lorenz Educational Publishers.

ISBN: 1–8885564–00–7

Library of Congress Card Catalog Card Number: 94–77242
Manufactured in the United States of America.
567890654321

The Tragedy of Macbeth

Contents

Introduction	iv
Characters	1
Act One	2
Act Two	42
Act Three	70
Act Four	108
Act Five	150
Glossary	183

Introduction

This volume of William Shakespeare's *The Tragedy of Macbeth* consists of two versions of the play. The first is the original, based on the *Globe* edition of 1860, which was in turn based on the Folio of 1623. The second is a translation of that version into contemporary English. In both versions spelling and punctuation have been updated, and the names of the characters have been spelled out in full for easier reading. Insights from modern scholars have been included in both versions.

The translation of *Macbeth* is not meant to take the place of the original. Instead, it is an alternative to the notes usually included in modern editions. In many cases these notes interfere with the reading of the play. Whether alongside or below the original text, the notes break the rhythm of reading and frequently force the reader to turn back to an earlier page or jump ahead to a later one. Having a translation that runs parallel to the original, line for line, allows the reader to move easily from Elizabethan to contemporary English and back again. It's simply a better way to introduce Shakespeare.

Also, this translation is suitable for performance, where notes are not available to the audience. Admittedly, a well-directed and well-acted production can do much to clarify Shakespeare's language. And yet, there will be numerous references and lines whose meanings are not accessible on a first hearing. What, for instance, does Banquo mean when he says that he will keep his "bosom franchised"?

Shakespeare's Language

Shakespeare's language does present problems for modern readers. After all, four centuries separate us from him. During this time words have acquired new meanings or have dropped from the language altogether, and sentence structures have become less fluid. But these are solvable problems.

First of all, most of the words that Shakespeare used are still current. For those words whose meanings have changed and for those words no longer in the language, modern equivalents are found in this translation. For a small number of words— chiefly names of places, biblical and mythological characters, and formal titles—a glossary can be found on page 183.

The meaning of words is one problem. The position of words is another.

Today, the order of words in declarative sentences is almost fixed. The subject comes first, then the verb, and finally, if there is one, the object. In Shakespeare's time, the order of words, particularly in poetic drama, was more fluid. Shakespeare has Macbeth say,

So foul and fair a day I have not seen.

Whereas we would usually arrange the words in this order,

I have not seen so foul and fair a day.

Later in the play, Macbeth says,

Look on it again, I dare not.

We would probably say,

I dare not look on it again.

This does not mean that Shakespeare never uses words in what we consider normal order. As often as not, he does. Here, for instance, are Macbeth and Banquo in conversation,

MACBETH   Your children shall be kings.
BANQUO   You shall be king.

When Shakespeare does invert the order of words, he does so for a reason or for a variety of reasons—to create a rhythm, to emphasize a word, to achieve a rhyme. Whether a play is in verse, as most of this play is, or in prose, it is still written in sentences. And that means that, despite the order, all the words needed to make complete sentences are there. If you are puzzled by a sentence, first look for the subject and then try rearranging the words in the order that you would normally use. It takes a little practice, but you will be surprised how quickly you acquire the skill.

Shakespeare sometimes separates sentence parts—subject and verb, for example—that would normally be run together. Here are some lines describing Macbeth in battle,

For brave Macbeth—well he deserves that name—
Disdaining Fortune with his brandished steel,
Which smoked with bloody execution,
Like Valor's darling, carved out his path.

Between the subject, *Macbeth,* and the verb, *carved out,* come some clauses and phrases that interrupt the normal sequence. Again, look for the subject and then the verb and put the two together. You'll find, however, that your rearranged sentence, while clear, is not as rhythmical as Shakespeare's.

Stage Directions

In drama written for the modern stage, the playwright usually provides detailed directions for the actors—how to move and speak, what emotions to convey to an audience. In the plays of Shakespeare, stage directions are sparse. One reason for this could be that Shakespeare was a member and an owner of the company for which he wrote these plays. He was on hand to tell the other actors how to say a line or what gesture to use. Even so, the dialogue itself offers clues to actions or gestures. For example, Macbeth, in Act Two, imagines he sees a dagger suspended in the air in front of him. He says,

> I see you still, in a form as palpable,
> As this which now I draw.

At this point, Macbeth probably draws a real dagger. Again, in Act One, Lady Macbeth greets Duncan at the entrance to her castle. Duncan says,

> By your leave, hostess.

And they enter the castle. At this point, Duncan may take Lady Macbeth's arm, or possibly give her a kiss. The line calls for some gesture, but, of course, lacking a written direction, one can't be sure exactly what it is.

Reading the printed play, you must be alert to whom a line of dialogue is addressed. For example, after meeting the three witches who predict that Macbeth shall be king, Banquo addresses Macbeth and asks him,

> Good sir, why do you jump and seem to fear
> Things that sound so good?

Then, turning to the three witches, he continues,

> In the name of truth,
> Are you a fantasy or that indeed
> Which you seem to be?

But there is no stage direction to mark this change. You have to try to picture the characters in your mind.

Solo Speeches

There is another difference between the plays of Shakespeare and most modern ones—the solo speeches. These are the asides and the soliloquies in which a character reveals what is on his or her mind. Modern dramatists seem to feel that the solo speech is artificial and unrealistic. Oddly enough, modern novelists frequently use a variety of the solo speech, and some critics feel that this convention has given the novel extra power and depth, allowing it to probe deeply into the motives of its characters. One thing is certain—Shakespeare's plays without the solo speeches would not be as powerful as they are.

The Tragedy of
Macbeth

Characters

Three WITCHES, the WEIRD SISTERS
DUNCAN, King of Scotland
MALCOLM, his older son
DONALBAIN, Duncan's younger son
MACBETH, Thane of Glamis
LADY MACBETH, his wife
SEYTON, an officer, attending on Macbeth
Three MURDERERS, in Macbeth's service
DOCTOR, attending on Lady Macbeth
GENTLEWOMAN, attending on Lady Macbeth
BANQUO, general, with Macbeth, of Scottish army
FLEANCE, his son
MACDUFF, Scottish noble
LADY MACDUFF, his wife
SON, their son
LENNOX
ROSS
ANGUS   } Scottish nobles
MENTEITH
CAITHNESS
SIWARD, commander of the English army
YOUNG SIWARD, his son
CAPTAIN, officer in Duncan's army
OLD MAN
ENGLISH DOCTOR
HECATE
PORTER
Three MESSENGERS, Three SERVANTS, a LORD,
    ATTENDANTS, APPARITIONS

Act One

Scene 1 [*Scotland. An open place*]

Thunder and lightning. Enter three WITCHES

FIRST WITCH When shall we three meet again
    In thunder, lightning, or in rain?

SECOND WITCH When the hurlyburly's done
    When the battle's lost and won.

THIRD WITCH That will be ere the set of sun.   5

FIRST WITCH Where the place?

SECOND WITCH Upon the heath.

THIRD WITCH There to meet with Macbeth.

FIRST WITCH I come, Graymalkin.

SECOND WITCH Paddock calls.   10

THIRD WITCH Anon.

ALL Fair is foul, and foul is fair.
    Hover through the fog and filthy air.

                           Exeunt

Scene 2 [*A camp near Forres*]

Alarum within. Enter DUNCAN, MALCOLM, DONALBAIN,
      LENNOX, *with* ATTENDANTS, *meeting a bleeding* SERGEANT

DUNCAN What bloody man is that? He can report,
    As seemeth by his plight, of the revolt
    The newest state.

MALCOLM This is the sergeant
    Who like a good and hardy soldier fought   5
    'Gainst my captivity. Hail, brave friend!

Act One

Scene 1 [*Scotland. An open place*]

Thunder and lightning. Enter three WITCHES

FIRST WITCH When shall we three meet again?

    In thunder, lightning, or in rain?

SECOND WITCH When the hurlyburly's done,

    When the battle's lost and won.

THIRD WITCH That's before the set of sun.   5

FIRST WITCH Where's the place?

SECOND WITCH Upon the heath.

THIRD WITCH There to meet Macbeth.

FIRST WITCH I come, my gray cat.

SECOND WITCH The demon toad calls.   10

THIRD WITCH At once, I'm coming.

ALL Fair is foul, and foul is fair.

    Hover through the fog and filthy air.

They exit

Scene 2 [*A camp near Forres*]

Trumpet fanfare off-stage. Enter DUNCAN, MALCOLM, DONALBAIN,

      LENNOX, *with* ATTENDANTS, *meeting a bleeding* CAPTAIN

DUNCAN Who is that wounded man? From the looks of him,

    He can report on the current state

    Of the revolt.

MALCOLM This is the captain

    Who, like a good and hardy soldier, fought   5

    Against my captivity. Welcome, brave friend!

Say to the King the knowledge of the broil

As thou didst leave it.

SERGEANT Doubtful it stood,

As two spent swimmers that do cling together   10

And choke their art. The merciless Macdonwald

(Worthy to be a rebel, for to that

The multiplying villainies of nature

Do swarm upon him) from the Western Isles

Of kerns and gallowglasses is supplied;   15

And Fortune, on his damned quarrel smiling,

Showed like a rebel's whore. But all's too weak;

For brave Macbeth (well he deserves that name),

Disdaining Fortune, with his brandished steel,

Which smoked with bloody execution   20

(Like valor's minion), carved out his passage

Till he faced the slave;

Which ne'er shook hands nor bade farewell to him

Till he unseamed him from the nave to the chops

And fixed his head upon our battlements.   25

DUNCAN O valiant cousin! Worthy gentleman!

SERGEANT As whence the sun 'gins his reflection

Shipwracking storms and direful thunders break,

So from that spring whence comfort seemed to come

Discomfort swells. Mark, King of Scotland, mark.   30

No sooner justice had, with valor armed,

Compelled these skipping kerns to trust their heels

But the Norweyan lord, surveying vantage,

With furbished arms and new supplies of men,

Began a fresh assault.   35

Tell the king what you know of the battle
As you left the field.

CAPTAIN Doubtful it stood,

Like two spent swimmers that cling together   10
And hinder each other's skill. The merciless Macdonwald—
The perfect rebel to whom
The vices of human nature
Do breed and swarm—had from the Western Isles
With infantry and cavalry been supplied;   15
And Fortune, like a tease, seemed to smile
On his damned cause. But all to no avail,
For brave Macbeth—well he deserves that name—
Disdaining Fortune with his brandished steel,
Which smoked with bloody execution,   20
Like Valor's darling, carved out his path
Till he faced the foe;
Then never shook hands nor bid farewell to him
Till he ripped him open from the belly to the jaw,
And stuck his head upon our battlements.   25

DUNCAN O valiant cousin, worthy gentleman!

CAPTAIN From the east, where the sun begins the day,

And shipwrecking storms and terrifying thunders break,
So from that spring where comfort seemed to come,
Pain swelled forth. Listen, King of Scotland: 30
No sooner had Justice, armed with Valor,
Compelled these fleeing troops to take to their heels,
But the Norwegian lord, seeing his chance,
With strengthened arms and new supplies of men,
Began a fresh assault.   35

DUNCAN Dismayed not this

    Our captains, Macbeth and Banquo?

SERGEANT Yes,

    As sparrows eagles, or the hare the lion.

    If I say sooth, I must report there were

    As cannons overcharged with double cracks, so they   40

    Doubly redoubled strokes upon the foe.

    Except they meant to bathe in reeking wounds,

    Or memorize another Golgotha,

    I cannot tell—

    But I am faint; my gashes cry for help.   45

DUNCAN So well thy words become thee as thy wounds;

    They smack of honor both. Go get him surgeons.

Exit SERGEANT, *attended*

Enter ROSS *and* ANGUS

    Who comes here?

MALCOLM The worthy Thane of Ross.

LENNOX What a haste looks through his eyes! So should he look   50

    That seems to speak things strange.

ROSS God save the King!

DUNCAN Whence camest thou, worthy thane?

ROSS From Fife, great King.

    Where Norweyan banners flout the sky   55

    And fan our people cold. Norway himself,

    With terrible numbers,

    Assisted by that most disloyal traitor

    The Thane of Cawdor, began a dismal conflict,

    Till that Bellona's bridegroom, lapped in proof,   60

    Confronted him with self-comparisons,

    Point against point, rebellious arm 'gainst arm,

DUNCAN Did this not dismay

    Our captains, Macbeth and Banquo?

CAPTAIN Yes, as sparrows fear eagles or the hare the lion.

    To tell the truth, I must report they were

    As cannons overfed with double charges;   40

    So they doubly redoubled strokes upon the foe.

    Unless they meant to bathe in steaming wounds

    Or else create another Golgotha,

    I cannot tell—

    But I am faint, my wounds cry for help.   45

DUNCAN So well your words become you as your wounds,

    They taste of honor both. Go get him surgeons.

Exit CAPTAIN, *attended*

Enter ROSS *and* ANGUS

    Who comes here?

MALCOLM The worthy Thane of Ross.

LENNOX What urgency is in his eyes!   50

    Like someone about to speak of unknown things.

ROSS God save the King!

DUNCAN Where do you come from, worthy thane?

ROSS From Fife, great King,

    Where Norwegian banners insult our sky   55

    And turn our people cold with fear.

    Norway's king himself, with massive throngs,

    Assisted by that most disloyal traitor,

    The Thane of Cawdor, threatened disaster,

    Till Macbeth, like War's bridegroom, in tested armor   60

    Faced him with equal strength and courage,

    Blow for blow, rebellious arm against arm,

Curbing his lavish spirit; and to conclude,

The victory fell on us.

DUNCAN Great happiness!   65

ROSS That now

Sweno, the Norways' king, craves composition;

Nor would we deign him burial of his men

Till he disbursed, at Saint Colme's Inch,

Ten thousand dollars to our general use.   70

DUNCAN No more that Thane of Cawdor shall deceive

Our bosom interest. Go pronounce his present death

And with his former title greet Macbeth.

ROSS I'll see it done.

DUNCAN What he hath lost noble Macbeth hath won.   75

Exeunt

Scene 3 [*A blasted heath*]

Thunder. Enter the three WITCHES

FIRST WITCH Where hast thou been, sister?

SECOND WITCH Killing swine.

THIRD WITCH Sister, where thou?

FIRST WITCH A sailor's wife had chestnuts in her lap

And munched and munched and munched. "Give me," quoth I.   5

"Aroint thee, witch!" the rump-fed ronyon cried.

Her husband's to Aleppo gone, master of the Tiger;

But in a sieve I'll thither sail

And, like a rat without a tail,

I'll do, I'll do, and I'll do.   10

SECOND WITCH I'll give thee a wind.

FIRST WITCH Thou are kind.

THIRD WITCH And I another.

FIRST WITCH I myself have all the other,

Checking his fierce attack; and, to conclude,

The victory fell to us.

DUNCAN Great happiness!   65

ROSS So now Sweno,

King of Norway, begs for terms of peace;

But we would not allow him burial for his men

Till he gave us, at Saint Colme's Isle,

Ten thousand dollars for our general use.   70

DUNCAN No more shall that Thane of Cawdor deceive

Our affection and trust. Go pronounce his present death,

And with his former title greet Macbeth.

ROSS I'll see it done.

DUNCAN What he has lost, noble Macbeth has won.   75

They exit

Scene 3 [*A heath*]

Thunder. Enter the three WITCHES

FIRST WITCH Where have you been, sister?

SECOND WITCH Killing swine.

THIRD WITCH And you, sister?

FIRST WITCH A sailor's wife had chestnuts in her lap,

And munched, and munched, and munched. "Give me," said I.   5

"Be gone, witch!" the fat-rumped wretch cries.

Her husband's to Aleppo gone, captain of the *Tiger;*

But in a sieve I too shall sail,

And like a rat without a tail,

I'll take revenge, revenge, revenge.   10

SECOND WITCH I'll give you a wind.

FIRST WITCH You are kind.

THIRD WITCH And I another.

FIRST WITCH But I already have them all,

And the very ports they blow, 15

And all the quarters that they know

In the shipman's card.

I will drain him dry as hay.

Sleep shall neither night nor day

Hang upon his penthouse lid. 20

He shall live a man forbid.

Weary seven nights, nine times nine,

Shall he dwindle, peak, and pine.

Though his bark cannot be lost,

Yet it shall be tempest-tossed. 25

Look what I have.

SECOND WITCH Show me! Show me!

FIRST WITCH Here I have a pilot's thumb,

Wracked as homeward he did come.

Drum within.

THIRD WITCH A drum, a drum! 30

Macbeth doth come.

ALL The Weird Sisters, hand in hand,

Posters of the sea and land,

Thus do go about, about,

Thrice to thine, and thrice to mine, 35

And thrice again, to make up nine.

Peace! The charm's wound up.

Enter MACBETH *and* BANQUO

MACBETH So foul and fair a day I have not seen.

BANQUO How far is it called to Forres? What are these,

So withered, and so wild in their attire, 40

That look not like the inhabitants of the earth,

And yet are on it? Live you? Or are you aught

10

Even know the ports from which they blow,   15
And all the quarters
On the sailor's compass.
I'll drain the man dry as hay;
He shall sleep neither night nor day.
Sleep shall not hang on his eyelids,   20
He will be a man accursed,
Weary seven nights nine times nine,
Shall he dwindle, waste, and pine.
Though his ship cannot be lost,
Yet it shall be tempest-tossed.   25
Look what I have here.

SECOND WITCH Show me, show me!

FIRST WITCH Here I have a pilot's thumb,
Wrecked as homeward he did come.

Drums off-stage.

THIRD WITCH A drum, a drum!   30
Macbeth does come.

ALL The Weird Sisters, hand in hand,
Swift travelers of sea and land,
Thus do go about, about,
Three times here and three times there,   35
And three again to make up nine.
Peace! The charm's wound up.

Enter MACBETH *and* BANQUO

MACBETH So foul and fair a day I have not seen.

BANQUO How far do you think to Forres? What are these,
So withered and so wild in their attire   40
That look not like the inhabitants of the earth,
And yet are on it? Live you? Or are you such

That man may question? You seem to understand me,

By each at once her choppy finger laying

Upon her skinny lips. You should be women, 45

And yet your beards forbid me to interpret

That you are so.

MACBETH Speak, if you can. What are you?

FIRST WITCH All hail, Macbeth! Hail to thee, Thane of Glamis!

SECOND WITCH All hail, Macbeth! Hail to thee, Thane of Cawdor! 50

THIRD WITCH All hail, Macbeth, that shalt be King hereafter!

BANQUO Good sir, why do you start and seem to fear

Things that do sound so fair? In the name of truth,

Are ye fantastical, or that indeed

Which outwardly ye show? My noble partner 55

You greet with present grace and great prediction

Of noble having and of royal hope,

That he seems rapt withal. To me you speak not.

If you can look into the seeds of time

And say which grain will grow and which will not, 60

Speak then to me, who neither beg nor fear

Your favors nor your hate.

FIRST WITCH Hail!

SECOND WITCH Hail!

THIRD WITCH Hail! 65

FIRST WITCH Lesser than Macbeth, and greater.

SECOND WITCH Not so happy, yet much happier.

THIRD WITCH Thou shalt get kings, though you be none.

So all hail, Macbeth and Banquo!

FIRST WITCH Banquo and Macbeth, all hail! 70

MACBETH Stay, you imperfect speakers, tell me more!

By Sinel's death I know I am Thane of Glamis;

That man may question? You seem to understand me,

By each at once her chapped finger laying

Upon her skinny lips. You should be women,   45

And yet your beards make me hesitate to think

That you are so.

MACBETH Speak if you can. What are you?

FIRST WITCH All hail, Macbeth! Hail to you, Thane of Glamis!

SECOND WITCH All hail, Macbeth! Hail to you, Thane of Cawdor!   50

THIRD WITCH All hail, Macbeth! You shall be King hereafter!--

BANQUO Good sir, why do you jump and seem to fear

Things that sound so good? In the name of truth,

Are you a fantasy or that indeed

Which you seem to be? My noble partner   55

You greet with honors and great prediction

Of noble presence and of kingly hope

That leaves him dazed. To me you speak not.

If you can look into the seeds of time

And say which grain will grow and which will not,   60

Speak to me, who neither beg nor fear

Your favors or your hate.

FIRST WITCH Hail!

SECOND WITCH Hail!

THIRD WITCH Hail!   65

FIRST WITCH Lesser than Macbeth, and greater.

SECOND WITCH Not so favored, yet more favored.

THIRD WITCH You shall beget kings, though be none yourself.

So all hail, Macbeth and Banquo!

FIRST WITCH Banquo and Macbeth, all hail!   70

MACBETH Stay, you obscuring speakers, tell me more.

By Father's death, I know I am Thane of Glamis,

But how of Cawdor? The Thane of Cawdor lives,

A prosperous gentleman; and to be King

Stands not within the prospect of belief,   75

No more than to be Cawdor. Say from whence

You owe this strange intelligence, or why

Upon this blasted heath you stop our way,

With prophetic greetings. Speak, I charge you.

WITCHES vanish

BANQUO The earth hath bubbles, as the water has,   80

And these are of them. Whither are they vanished?

MACBETH Into the air, and what seemed corporal melted

As breath into the wind. Would they had stayed!

BANQUO Were such things here as we do speak about?

Or have we eaten on the insane root   85

That takes the reason prisoner?

MACBETH Your children shall be kings.

BANQUO You shall be King.

MACBETH And Thane of Cawdor too. Went it not so?

BANQUO To the selfsame tune and words. Who's here?   90

Enter ROSS and ANGUS

ROSS The King hath happily received, Macbeth,

The news of thy success; and when he reads

Thy personal venture in the rebels' fight,

His wonders and praises do contend

Which should be thine or his. Silenced with that,   95

In viewing o'er the rest of the selfsame day,

He finds thee in the stout Norweyan ranks,

Nothing afeard of what thyself didst make,

Strange images of death. As thick as hale

Came post with post, and every one did bear   100

But not of Cawdor. The Thane of Cawdor lives,

A prosperous gentleman; and to be King

Stands not within the realm of belief,   75

No more than to be Cawdor. Say from where

You get these strange ideas, or why

Upon this blasted heath you stop our way

With such prophetic greetings. Speak, I tell you.

                                                  WITCHES *vanish*

BANQUO   The earth spawns illusions as the sea does,   80

    And these are of that kind. Still, where did they vanish?

MACBETH   Into the air, and what seemed solid melted,

    As breath in a wind. Would they had stayed!

BANQUO   Were such creatures here as we were speaking with?

    Or have we eaten some poison plant   85

    That makes the mind a slave?

MACBETH   Your children shall be kings.

BANQUO   You shall be King.

MACBETH   And Thane of Cawdor too. Did they not say so?

BANQUO   That's exactly the tune and the words. Who's here?   90

                          Enter ROSS *and* ANGUS

ROSS   The King has happily received, Macbeth,

    The news of your success; and when he considers

    Your brave risk in the rebels' fight,

    The wonder he feels rivals his wish to praise,

    Knowing that either is not enough. Silenced by that,   95

    In looking over this same day,

    He finds you in the midst of the Norwegian foes,

    Unafraid of what you have caused,

    Death in dreadful forms. As fast as one could count

    Came messenger after messenger, and every one did bear   100

Thy praises in his kingdom's great defense

And poured them down before him.

ANGUS We are sent

    To give thee from our royal master thanks;

    Only to herald thee into his sight,   105

    Not pay thee.

ROSS And for an earnest of a greater honor,

    He bade me, from him, call thee Thane of Cawdor;

    In which addition, hail, most worthy Thane!

    For it is thine.   110

BANQUO What, can the devil speak true?

MACBETH The Thane of Cawdor lives. Why do you dress me

    In borrowed robes?

ANGUS Who was the Thane lives yet,

    But under heavy judgment bears that life   115

    Which he deserves to lose. Whether he was combined

    With those of Norway, or did line the rebel

    With hidden help and vantage, or that with both

    He labored in his country's wrack, I know not;

    But treasons capital, confessed and proved,   120

    Have overthrown him.

MACBETH [*Aside*] Glamis, and Thane of Cawdor!

    The greatest is behind. [*To* ROSS *and* ANGUS]

    Thanks for your pains. [*Aside to* BANQUO]

    Do you not hope your children shall be kings,   125

    When those that gave the Thane of Cawdor to me

    Promised no less to them?

BANQUO [*Aside to* MACBETH] That, trusted home,

    Might yet enkindle you unto the crown,

Your praises in his kingdom's great defense,

And poured them down before him.

ANGUS We are sent

To give you, from our royal master, thanks;

Only to bring you to his sight,   105

Not ourselves to reward you.

ROSS And as a pledge of a greater honor,

He told me, from him, to call you Thane of Cawdor;

By that name, hail, most worthy Thane!

The title's now yours.   110

BANQUO [*Aside*] What, can the devil speak the truth?

MACBETH The Thane of Cawdor lives. Why do you dress me

In borrowed robes?

ANGUS He that was the thane lives yet,

But under sentence of his life,   115

Which he deserves to lose. Whether he was allied

With those of Norway, or did conspire with them

To give help and advantage, or did both

To work his country's ruin, I know not;

But treasons that are capital crimes, confessed, and proved   120

Have finished him.

MACBETH [*Aside*] Glamis, and now Thane of Cawdor;

What's most is already done. [*To* ROSS *and* ANGUS]

Thanks for your pains. [*Aside to* BANQUO]

Do you not hope your children shall be kings,   125

When those that gave the Thane of Cawdor to me

Promised no less to them?

BANQUO [*Aside to* MACBETH] That, taken seriously,

Might fire your hopes for the crown,

Beside the Thane of Cawdor. But 'tis strange! 130
And oftentimes, to win us to our harm,
The instruments of darkness tell us truths,
Win us with honest trifles, to betray us
In deepest consequence.
[*To* ANGUS *and* ROSS] Cousins, a word, I pray you. 135
MACBETH [*Aside*] Two truths are told,
As happy prologues to the swelling act
On the imperial theme. [*To* ROSS *and* ANGUS] I thank you,
Gentlemen.
[*Aside*] This supernatural soliciting 140
Cannot be ill; cannot be good. If ill,
Why hath it given me earnest of success,
Commencing in a truth? I am Thane of Cawdor.
If good, why do I yield to that suggestion
Whose horrid image doth unfix my hair 145
And make my seated heart knock at my ribs
Against the use of nature? Present fears
Are less than horrible imaginings.
My thought, whose murder yet is but fantastical,
Shakes so my single state of man that function 150
Is smothered in surmise and nothing is
But what is not.
BANQUO Look how our partner's rapt.
MACBETH [*Aside*] If chance will have me king. Why, chance
may crown me, 155
Without my stir.
BANQUO New honors come upon him,
Like our strange garments, cleave not to their mould

Besides the Thane of Cawdor. It's strange, but 130

Oftentimes, to entice us to our harm,

The agents of evil tell us truths,

Win us with little things, only to fool us

In matters of great importance.

[*To* ANGUS *and* ROSS] Comrades, a word with you. 135

MACBETH [*Aside*] Two truths are told,

As happy prologues to the unfolding act

On the imperial theme. [*To* ROSS *and* ANGUS] I thank you,
gentlemen.

[*Aside*] This supernatural influence, 140

Can it be bad, can it be good? If bad,

Why has it given me proof of success,

Beginning in a truth? I am Thane of Cawdor.

If good, why do I yield to that suggestion

Whose horrid image makes my hair stand on end, 145

And makes my firm heart pound against my ribs

In this unnatural way? Present fears

Are less than horrible imaginings.

My thought, in which murder is only imagined,

Shakes so my weak and human state that action 150

Is blocked by speculation and nothing is

But what is not.

BANQUO [*Aside*] Look, how our partner muses.

MACBETH [*Aside*] If luck will make me king, why luck
may crown me, 155

Without my stirring.

BANQUO New honors come upon him,

And like new clothes, do not fit

But with the aid of use.

MACBETH [*Aside*] Come what may,   160

    Time and the hour runs through the roughest day.

BANQUO Worthy Macbeth, we stay upon your leisure.

MACBETH Give me your favor. My dull brain was wrought

    With things forgotten. Kind gentlemen, your pains

    Are registered where every day I turn   165

    The leaf to read them. Let us toward the King.

    [*Aside to* BANQUO] Think upon what hath chanced; and,

        at more time,

    The interim having weighed it, let us speak

    Our free hearts each to other.   170

BANQUO [*Aside to* MACBETH] Very gladly.

MACBETH [*Aside to* BANQUO] Till then, enough. Come, friends.

                             Exeunt

Scene 4   [*Forres. The Palace*]

Flourish. Enter DUNCAN, LENNOX, MALCOLM, DONALBAIN, *and*
        ATTENDANTS

DUNCAN Is execution done on Cawdor? Are not

    Those in commission yet returned?

MALCOLM My liege,

    They are not yet come back. But I have spoke

    With one that saw him die; who did report   5

    That very frankly he confessed his treasons,

    Implored your Highness' pardon, and set forth

    A deep repentance. Nothing in his life

    Became him like the leaving it. He died

    As one that had been studied in his death   10

    To throw away the dearest thing he owned

Without some wear.

MACBETH [*Aside*] Come what may,   160

    Time brings an end to even the roughest day.

BANQUO Worthy Macbeth, we await you.

MACBETH Pardon me, my dull brain dwelt

    With things long past. Kind gentlemen, your patience

    Is recorded every day I read   165

    My book of debts to pay. Let us forward to the King.

    [*Aside to* BANQUO] Think about what has happened; and,

        when there's time,

    Having weighed the matter, let us speak

    Our free hearts each to the other.   170

BANQUO [*Aside to* MACBETH] Very gladly.

MACBETH [*Aside to* BANQUO] Till then, enough. Come, friends.

                    They exit

Scene 4 [*Forres. The Palace*]

Trumpet fanfare. Enter DUNCAN, LENNOX, MALCOLM, DONALBAIN, *and*
        ATTENDANTS

DUNCAN Has Cawdor yet been put to death? Where are

    Those that were given this charge?

MALCOLM My lord,

    They have not yet come back. But I did speak

    With one that saw him die, who did report   5

    That Cawdor frankly confessed his treasons,

    Implored your Highness' pardon, and expressed

    A deep repentance. Nothing in his life

    So became him like the leaving it. He died

    As one who had rehearsed his death,   10

    To throw away the dearest thing he owned

As 'twere a careless trifle.

DUNCAN   There's no art

To find the mind's construction in the face.

He was a gentleman on whom I built   15

An absolute trust.

            Enter MACBETH, BANQUO, ROSS, *and* ANGUS

O worthiest cousin,

The sin of my ingratitude even now

Was heavy on me! Thou art so far before

That swiftest wing of recompense is slow   20

To overtake thee. Would thou hadst less deserved,

That the proportion both of thanks and payment

Might have been mine! Only I have left to say,

More is thy due than more than all can pay.

MACBETH   The service and the loyalty I owe,   25

In doing it pays itself. Your Highness' part

Is to receive our duties; and our duties

Are to your throne and state children and servants,

Which do but what they should by doing everything

Safe toward your love and honor.   30

DUNCAN   Welcome hither.

I have begun to plant thee and will labor

To make thee full of growing. Noble Banquo,

That hast no less deserved, nor must be known

No less to have done so, let me infold thee   35

And hold thee to my heart.

BANQUO   There if I grow,

The harvest is your own.

DUNCAN   My plenteous joys,

Wanton in fullness, seek to hide themselves   40

As if it were a worthless trifle.

DUNCAN There's no way

    To read a man's character in his face.

    He was a gentleman on whom I built   15

    An absolute trust.

          Enter MACBETH, BANQUO, ROSS, *and* ANGUS

    Worthiest cousin!

    The sin of my ingratitude even now

    Weighs heavy on me! You are so far ahead

    That the swiftest wing of recompense is slow   20

    To overtake you. If only you had deserved less,

    Then the debt of thanks and payment

    Might have been mine. I can only say,

    You're due more than I can ever pay.

MACBETH The service and the loyalty I give   25

    Are their own reward. Your Highness' part

    Is to receive our duties, and our duties

    Are to your throne and state as children and servants,

    Which do only what they should by doing all

    To ensure your love and honor.   30

DUNCAN Come here,

    I have begun to nurture you, and will labor

    To make you bloom. Noble Banquo,

    Who have deserved no less, nor must be known

    No less to have done so, let me hug you close   35

    And hold you to my heart.

BANQUO There if I grow,

    The harvest is your own.

DUNCAN My plentiful joys,

    Overflowing everywhere, disguise themselves   40

In drops of sorrow. Sons, kinsmen, thanes,
And you whose places are the nearest, know
We will establish our estate upon
Our eldest, Malcolm, whom we name hereafter
The Prince of Cumberland; which honor must   45
Not unaccompanied invest him only,
But signs of nobleness, like stars, shall shine
On all deservers. From hence to Inverness,
And bind us further to you.
MACBETH The rest is labor, which is not used for you!   50
I'll be myself the harbinger, and make joyful
The hearing of my wife with your approach;
So, humbly take my leave.
DUNCAN My worthy Cawdor!
MACBETH [*Aside*] The Prince of Cumberland! That is a step   55
On which I must fall down, or else o'erleap,
For in my way it lies. Stars, hide your fires!
Let not light see my black and deep desires.
The eye wink at the hand; yet let that be,
Which the eye fears, when it is done, to see.   60

Exit

DUNCAN True, worthy Banquo: he is full so valiant
And in his commendations I am fed;
It is a banquet to me. Let's after him,
Whose care is gone before to bid us welcome.
It is a peerless kinsman.   65
Flourish.

Exeunt

As tears. Sons, kinsmen, thanes,

And you who are the nearest, know

We will settle the succession upon

Our eldest, Malcolm, whom we name hereafter

The Prince of Cumberland, which honor must   45

Not go unaccompanied,

But with titles, like stars, shall shine

On all who are deserving. [*To* MACBETH] From hence to Inverness,

And put us further in your debt.

MACBETH   Rest is but labor, when not done for you.   50

I'll myself be the messenger that brings my wife

The joyful news of your approach.

So, humbly take my leave.

DUNCAN   My worthy Cawdor!

MACBETH [*Aside*] The Prince of Cumberland! That is a step   55

On which I must fall down, or else leap over,

For it lies in my way. Stars, hide your fires,

Don't let the light see my black and deep desires;

Don't let the eye see what the hand would do;

Yet let the deed be done.   60

He exits

DUNCAN   True, worthy Banquo; he is so valiant,

That on his praises I am sated:

It's a banquet to me. Let's follow him,

Whose kindness goes ahead to bid us welcome.

He is a peerless kinsman.   65

Trumpet fanfare.

They exit

Scene 5 [*Inverness. Macbeth's castle*]

    Enter LADY MACBETH, *alone, with a letter*

LADY MACBETH [*reads*] "They met me in the day of success; and I have
learned by the perfectest report that they have more in them than mortal
knowledge. When I burned in desire to question them further,
they made themselves air, into which they vanished. Whiles I stood
rapt in the wonder of it, came missives from the King, who all-hailed me   5
Thane of Cawdor, by which title, before, these Weird Sisters saluted me,
and referred me to the coming of a time with 'Hail, King that shalt be!'
This have I thought good to deliver thee, my dearest partner of greatness,
that thou might not lose the dues of rejoicing by being ignorant of what
greatness is promised thee. Lay it to thy heart, and farewell."   10

  Glamis thou art, and Cawdor, and shalt be
  What thou art promised. Yet I do fear thy nature.
  It is too full of the milk of human kindness
  To catch the nearest way. Thou wouldst be great;
  Are not without ambition, but without   15
  The illness should attend it. What thou wouldst highly,
  That wouldst thou holily; wouldst not play false,
  And yet wouldst wrongly win. Thou'ldst have, great Glamis
  That which cries "Thus thou must do," if thou have it;
  And that which rather thou dost fear to do   20
  Than wishest should be undone. Hie thee hither,
  That I may pour my spirits in thine ear
  And chastise with the valor of my tongue
  All that impedes thee from the golden round
  Which fate and metaphysical aid doth seem   25
  To have thee crowned withal.

Scene 5 [*Inverness. Macbeth's castle*]

              Enter LADY MACBETH, *alone, with a letter*

LADY MACBETH [*reads*] "They met me on my day of victory, and I have
learned from reliable sources that their knowledge transcends mere mortal
knowledge. Although I burned with desire to question them further,
they made themselves into air and vanished. While I stood there entranced,
messengers came from the King, who hailed me 'Thane of Cawdor,'   5
the same title used by those Weird Sisters who foretold a time when
'King you shall be!' This have I thought good to tell you,
my dearest partner in success, so that you'll not lose your
share of rejoicing by being ignorant of the brilliant future promised
you. Think about it, and farewell."   10

    Glamis you are and Cawdor, and shall be
    What you are promised. Yet I do fear your nature.
    It is too full of the milk of human kindness
    To seize the quickest way. You want to be great,
    And are not without ambition, but you lack   15
    The evil that must accompany it. What you wish for most,
    You would have honestly, would not play false,
    And yet would wrongly win. You would rather,
    Great Glamis, act from duty,
    And do what you fear to do,   20
    Than do what you should not. Come to me,
    That I may pour my resolve in your ear,
    And drive out with the valor of my tongue
    All that impedes you from the golden round,
    Which fate and the supernatural do seem   25
    To have you crowned with.

Enter MESSENGER

What is your tidings?

MESSENGER The King comes here tonight.

LADY MACBETH Thou'rt mad to say it!

Is not thy master with him? who, were't so,   30

Would have informed for preparation.

MESSENGER So please you, it is true. Our Thane is coming.

One of my fellows had the speed of him,

Who, almost dead for breath, had scarcely more

Than would make up his message.   35

LADY MACBETH Give him tending;

He brings great news.

Exit MESSENGER

The raven himself is horse

That croaks the fatal entrance of Duncan

Under my battlements. Come, you spirits   40

That tend on mortal thoughts, unsex me here,

And fill me, from the crown to the toe, top-full

Of direst cruelty! Make thick my blood;

Stop up the access and passage to remorse,

That no compunctious visiting of nature   45

Shake my fell purpose nor keep peace between

The effect and it! Come to my woman's breasts

And take my milk for gall, you murdering ministers,

Wherever in your sightless substances

You wait on nature's mischief! Come, thick night,   50

And pall thee in the dunnest smoke of hell,

That my keen knife see not the wound it makes,

Nor heaven peep through the blanket of the dark

To cry "Hold, hold!"

Enter MESSENGER

What news do you have?

MESSENGER The King comes here tonight.

LADY MACBETH You are mad to say it.

Is not your master with him, who, were it so,   30

Would have sent word so that I might prepare.

MESSENGER So please you, it is true; our thane is coming.

One of my fellows sped ahead of him,

And almost dead for want of breath,

Did deliver this message.   35

LADY MACBETH Go tend him;

He brings great news.

Exit MESSENGER

The raven himself is hoarse

That croaks the fatal entrance of Duncan

Under my battlements. Come, you spirits   40

That tend on deadly thoughts, unsex me here,

And fill me, from the crown to the toe, top-full

Of direst cruelty. Make thick my blood,

Stop up the access and passage to remorse,

So that no natural scruples of conscience   45

Shake my fierce purpose, nor keep peace between

The effect and it. Come to my woman's breasts

And change their milk to gall, you ministers of murder,

Wherever in your invisible substances

You wait on nature's mischief. Come, thick night,   50

And cover in the darkest smoke of hell

My sharp knife so that it sees not the wounds it makes,

Nor let heaven peep through the blanket of the dark,

To cry out "Stop, stop!"

Enter MACBETH

Great Glamis! Worthy Cawdor!   55

Greater than both, by the all-hail hereafter!

Thy letters have transported me beyond

This ignorant present, and I feel now

The future in the instant.

MACBETH My dearest love.   60

Duncan comes here tonight.

LADY MACBETH And when goes hence?

MACBETH Tomorrow, as he purposes.

LADY MACBETH O, never

Shall sun that morrow see!   65

Your face, my thane, is as a book where men

May read strange matters. To beguile the time,

Look like the time; bear welcome in your eye,

Your hand, your tongue; look like the innocent flower,

But be the serpent under it. He that's coming   70

Must be provided for; and you shall put

This night's great business into my dispatch,

Which shall to all our nights and days to come

Give solely sovereign sway and masterdom.

MACBETH We will speak further.   75

LADY MACBETH Only look up clear.

To alter favor ever is to fear.

Leave all the rest to me.

Exeunt

Enter MACBETH

Great Glamis! Worthy Cawdor!   55
Greater than both hereafter, all hail!
Your letters have transported me beyond
This ignorant present, and I feel now
The future in this instant.
MACBETH My dearest love,   60
Duncan comes here tonight.
LADY MACBETH And when does he leave?
MACBETH Tomorrow, as he intends.
LADY MACBETH O, never
Shall sun that morrow see!   65
Your face, my thane, is like a book where men
May read strange matters. To fool the world,
You must suit the occasion; bear welcome in your eye,
Your hand, your tongue; look like the innocent flower,
But be the serpent under it. He that's coming   70
Must be provided for; and you shall put
This night's great business under my care,
Which shall to all our nights and days to come
Give nothing but sovereign sway and mastery.
MACBETH We'll speak about it later.   75
LADY MACBETH Only look calm.
To seem odd is dangerous.
Leave all the rest to me.
                                                        They exit

Scene 6 [*Inverness. Before Macbeth's castle*]

Hautboys and torches. Enter DUNCAN, MALCOLM, DONALBAIN, ROSS,
      BANQUO, LENNOX, MACDUFF, ANGUS, *and* ATTENDANTS

DUNCAN This castle hath a pleasant seat. The air

  Nimbly and sweetly recommends itself

  Unto our gentle senses.

BANQUO This guest of summer,

  The temple-haunting martlet, does approve   5

  By his loved mansionry that the heaven's breath

  Smells wooingly here. No jutty, frieze,

  Buttress, nor coin of vantage, but this bird

  Hath made his pendent bed and procreant cradle.

  Where they most breed and haunt, I have observed,   10

  The air is delicate.

Enter LADY MACBETH

DUNCAN See, see, our honored hostess!

  The love that follows us sometime is our trouble,

  Which we still thank as love. Herein I teach you

  How you shall bid God yield us for your pains   15

  And thank us for your trouble.

LADY MACBETH All our service

  In every point twice done, and then done double,

  Were poor and single business to contend

  Against those honors deep and broad wherewith   20

  Your Majesty loads our house. For those of old,

  And the late dignities heaped upon them,

  We rest your hermits.

DUNCAN Where's the Thane of Cawdor?

  We coursed him at the heels and had a purpose   25

  To be his purveyor; but he rides well,

Scene 6 [*Inverness. Before Macbeth's castle*]

Oboes and torch bearers. Enter DUNCAN, MALCOLM, DONALBAIN, ROSS,
    BANQUO, LENNOX, MACDUFF, ANGUS, *and* ATTENDANTS

DUNCAN   This castle has a pleasing site. The air,

    With its freshness and sweetness, appeals

    To our senses and soothes them.

BANQUO   This guest of summer,

    The church-nesting martin, does prove   5

    By his loving nests here that the air has

    Heaven's freshness. In every projection,

    Corner, and nook, this bird

    Has made his hanging bed and spawning-cradle.

    Where they live and breed, I have observed,   10

    The air is delicate.

                  Enter LADY MACBETH

DUNCAN   See, see, our honored hostess.

    Our subjects' love is sometimes a bother,

    But still we are grateful. Let me show you

    How you shall ask God to reward your pains,   15

    And thank you for your trouble.

LADY MACBETH   All our service,

    Even if done twice, and then twice again,

    Would be poor and slight to compete

    Against those honors deep and broad with which   20

    Your Majesty loads our house. For those of old,

    And the new ones added to them,

    We remain duty-bound to pray for your well-being.

DUNCAN   Where's the Thane of Cawdor?

    We followed him closely and had hoped   25

    To be his herald, but he rides well,

And his great love, sharp as his spur, hath holp him
To his home before us. Fair and noble hostess,
We are your guests tonight.

LADY MACBETH Your servants ever   30
Have theirs, themselves, and what is theirs, in compt
To make their audit at your Highness' pleasure,
Still to return your own.

DUNCAN Give me your hand;
Conduct me to mine host. We love him highly   35
And shall continue our graces towards him.
By your leave, hostess.

Exeunt

Scene 7 [*Inverness. Macbeth's castle*]

Hautboys. Torches. Enter a SEWER, *and divers* SERVANTS *with dishes and*
service over the stage. Then enter MACBETH

MACBETH If it were done when 'tis done, then 'twere well
It were done quickly. If the assassination
Could trammel up the consequence, and catch,
With his surcease, success; that but this blow
Might be the be-all and the end-all here,   5
But here, upon this bank and shoal of time,
We'd jump the life to come. But in these cases
We still have judgment here, that we but teach
Bloody instructions, which being taught, return
To plague the inventor. This even-handed justice   10
Commends the ingredience of our poisoned chalice
To our lips. He's here in doubly trust:
First, as I am kinsman and his subject—
Strong both against the deed; then, as his host,
Who should against his murderer shut the door,   15

34

And spurred on by his love for you,

Had reached his home before us. Fair and noble hostess,

We are your guest tonight.

LADY MACBETH Your servants always   30

Hold themselves and what is theirs in trust to you,

To render it all at your Highness' pleasure,

Always to return what is your due.

DUNCAN Give me your hand.

Lead me to my host. We love him highly   35

And he shall continue in our graces.

Permit me, hostess.

They exit

Scene 7 [*Inverness. Macbeth's castle*]
Oboes and torch bearers. Enter and pass across the stage a STEWARD *and
        various* SERVANTS *with dishes of food. Then enter* MACBETH

MACBETH If it were finished when it was done, then it's best

That it be done quickly. If the assassination

Could itself net further consequences, and catch,

With this act, success; that this blow alone

Might be the be-all and end-all here,   5

Upon this bank and shore of time,

We'd risk the life to come. But in such cases

There is always a judgment in this life; we may teach

Others bloody lessons that, being taught,

Return to plague us. This even-handed justice   10

Prescribes the mixture of our own poisoned chalice

To our own lips. The King's here in double trust;

First, I am both his kinsman and his subject—

Strong bars against the deed; then, as his host,

Who should against his murderer shut the door,   15

Not bear the knife myself. Besides, this Duncan
Hath borne his faculties so meek, hath been
So clear in his great office, that his virtues
Will plead like angels, trumpet-tongued, against
The deep damnation of his taking-off;   20
And pity, like a naked new-born babe,
Striding the blast, or heaven's cherubin, horsed
Upon the sightless couriers of the air,
Shall blow the horrid deed in every eye,
That tears shall drown the wind. I have no spur   25
To prick the sides of my intent, but only
Vaulting ambition, which overleaps itself
And falls on the other side.

Enter LADY MACBETH

How now? What news?

LADY MACBETH He has almost supped. Why have you left the chamber? 30

MACBETH   Hath he asked for me?

LADY MACBETH   Know you not he has?

MACBETH   We will proceed no further in this business.
He hath honored me of late, and I have bought
Golden opinions from all sorts of people,   35
Which would be worn now in their newest gloss,
Not cast aside so soon.

LADY MACBETH   Was the hope drunk
Wherein you dressed yourself? Hath it slept since?
And wakes it now to look so green and pale   40
At what it did so freely? From this time
Such I account thy love. Art thou afeard
To be the same in thine own act and valor
As thou art in desire? Wouldst thou have that

Not bear the knife myself. Besides, this Duncan
Has borne his powers so gently, has been
So blameless in his great office, that his virtues
Will plead like angels, trumpet-tongued against
The deep damnation of his murder;   20
And pity, like a new-born babe
Riding the wind, or heaven's cherubim, horsed
Upon the invisible steeds of the air,
Shall blow the horrid deed in every eye,
That tears shall drown the wind. I have no spur   25
To goad the sides of my intent, but only
Vaulting ambition, which overleaps itself
And falls on the other side.

Enter LADY MACBETH

How now, what news?

LADY MACBETH The meal's nearly over. Why did you leave the room? 30

MACBETH Has he asked for me?

LADY MACBETH Don't you know that he has?

MACBETH We will proceed no further in this business.
He has honored me just now and has given me
A golden reputation among all sorts of people,   35
Which I should wear now in its new luster,
Not cast aside so soon.

LADY MACBETH Was the hope drunk
In which you dressed yourself? Has it slept since?
And does it wake now to look so green and pale   40
At dreams it once sought? From this time
That's how I describe your love. Are you afraid
To be the same in act and deed
As you are in your dreams? Would you have the crown,

Which thou esteem'st the ornament of life   45

And live a coward in thine own esteem,

Letting "I dare not" wait upon "I would,"

Like the poor cat in the adage?

MACBETH Prithee peace!

    I dare do all that may become a man.   50

    Who dares more is none.

LADY MACBETH What beast was't then

That made you break this enterprise to me?

When you durst do it, then you were a man;

And to be more than what you were, you would   55

Be so much more the man. Nor time nor place

Did then adhere, and yet you would make both.

They have made themselves, and that their fitness now

Does unmake you. I have given suck, and know

How tender 'tis to love the babe that milks me.   60

I would, while it was smiling in my face,

Have plucked my nipple from his boneless gums

And dashed the brains out, had I so sworn as you

Have done to this.

MACBETH If we should fail?   65

LADY MACBETH We fail?

But screw your courage to the sticking place,

And we'll not fail. When Duncan is asleep

(Whereto the rather shall his day's hard journey

Soundly invite him), his two chamberlains   70

Will I with wine and wassail so convince

That memory, the warder of the brain,

Shall be a fume, and the receipt of reason

A limbeck only. When in swinish sleep

Which you esteem the ornament of life,   45

Or live a coward in your own sight,

Letting "I dare not" follow upon "I would,"

Like the cat in the proverb afraid to wet its paws to get a fish.

MACBETH I beg you, peace.

I dare do all that suits a man;   50

He who dares more is none.

LADY MACBETH Was it a beast then

That made you propose this scheme to me?

When you dared to do it, then you were a man;

And to be more than what you were, you'd   55

Be so much more the man. Neither time nor place

Were then convenient, and yet you would make both so;

They are together now, and their very fitness

Has unmade you. I have suckled babes and know

How tender it is to love the child that milks me;   60

I would, while it was smiling in my face,

Have plucked my nipple from his boneless gums,

And dashed his brains out, had I so sworn

As you have done to this.

MACBETH If we should fail?   65

LADY MACBETH We fail?

Just pull taut the bowstring of your courage,

And we'll not fail. When Duncan is asleep

(As doubtless his day's hard journey shall

Soundly invite him), his two attendants   70

Will I with wine and liquor so overpower

That their memory, guardian of the brain,

Shall turn to smoke, and reason to drops of vapor

In a heated skull. And while their besotted natures

Their drenched natures lie as in a death, 75

What cannot you and I perform upon

The unguarded Duncan? What not put upon

His spongy officers, who shall bear the guilt

Of our great quell?

MACBETH Bring forth men-children only; 80

For thy undaunted mettle should compose

Nothing but males. Will it not be received,

When we have marked with blood those sleepy two

Of his own chamber and used their very daggers,

That they have done it? 85

LADY MACBETH Who dares receive it other,

As we shall make our griefs and clamor roar

Upon his death?

MACBETH I am settled and bend up

Each corporal agent to this terrible feat, 90

Away, and mock the time with fairest show;

False face must hide what the false heart doth know.

Exeunt

Lie drenched in swinish sleep, as in a death,   75
What cannot you and I do
To the unguarded Duncan? And what cannot we blame
Upon his sodden officers, who shall bear the guilt
Of our great kill?

MACBETH Bring forth men-children only;   80
For your undaunted spirit should produce
Nothing but males. Will it not be thought,
When we have marked with blood those sleeping
Guardians of the king and used their own daggers,
That they have done it?   85

LADY MACBETH Who would dare believe otherwise,
As we shall make our griefs and anguish roar
Upon his death?

MACBETH I am resolute and taut,
Each bodily faculty bent to this terrible feat.   90
Leave, go fool the world with fairest show;
False face must hide what false heart does know.

They exit

Act Two

Scene 1 [*Inverness. The courtyard of Macbeth's castle*]

Enter BANQUO, *preceded by* FLEANCE *carrying a torch*

BANQUO How goes the night, boy?

FLEANCE The moon is down; I have not heard the clock.

BANQUO And she goes down at twelve.

FLEANCE I take it, 'tis later, sir.

BANQUO Hold, take my sword. There's husbandry in heaven;   5

Their candles are all out. Take thee that too.

A heavy summons lies like lead upon me,

And yet I would not sleep. Merciful powers,

Restrain in me the cursed thoughts that nature

Gives way to in repose!   10

Enter MACBETH *and a* SERVANT *with a torch*

Give me my sword.

Who's there?

MACBETH A friend.

BANQUO What, sir, not yet at rest? The King's abed.

He hath been in unusual pleasure and   15

Sent forth great largess to your offices.

This diamond he greets your wife withal

By the name of the most kind hostess, and shut up

In measureless content.

MACBETH Being unprepared,   20

Our will became the servant to defect,

Which else should free have wrought.

BANQUO All's well.

42

Act Two

Scene 1 [*Inverness. The courtyard of Macbeth's Castle*]

> *Enter* BANQUO, *preceded by* FLEANCE *carrying a torch*

BANQUO   What time is it, my boy?

FLEANCE   The moon is down, but I have not heard the clock.

BANQUO   And the moon goes down at twelve.

FLEANCE   Then it must be later, sir.

BANQUO   Here, take my sword. Heaven's stingy tonight;   5

    All her candles are out. Take this too.

    Sleep lies heavy upon me like lead,

    And yet I cannot close my eyes. Merciful powers,

    Restrain in me those evil thoughts that nature

    Releases in repose!   10

> *Enter* MACBETH *and a* SERVANT *with a torch*

    Give me my sword!

    Who's there?

MACBETH   A friend.

BANQUO   What, sir, not yet at rest? The King's in bed.

    He has been well pleased and has   15

    Sent many gifts to all your servants.

    This diamond he sends your wife, our

    Kind hostess, and ends his day

    In immeasurable contentment.

MACBETH   Being unprepared,   20

    Our wish to please the King fell short of what

    We would have done had we the time.

BANQUO   Everything went well.

I dreamt last night of the three Weird Sisters.

To you they have showed some truth. 25

MACBETH I think not of them.

Yet when we can entreat an hour to serve,

We would spend it in some words upon that business,

If you would grant the time.

BANQUO At your kindest leisure. 30

MACBETH If you shall cleave to my consent, when 'tis,

It shall make honor for you.

BANQUO So I lose none

In seeking to augment it but still keep

My bosom franchised and allegiance clear, 35

I shall be counseled.

MACBETH Good repose the while!

BANQUO Thanks, sir. The like to you!

Exeunt BANQUO *and* FLEANCE

MACBETH Go bid thy mistress, when my drink is ready,

She strike upon the bell. Get thee to bed. 40

Exit SERVANT

Is this a dagger which I see before me,

The handle toward my hand? Come, let me clutch thee!

I have thee not, and yet I see thee still.

Art thou not, fatal vision, sensible

To feeling as to sight? Or art thou but 45

A dagger of the mind, a false creation,

Proceeding from the heat-oppressed brain?

I see thee yet, in form as palpable

As this which now I draw.

Thou marshall'st me the way that I was going, 50

And such an instrument I was to use.

Act Two, Scene 1

I dreamed last night of the three Weird Sisters.
They have shown some truth to you. 25

MACBETH I haven't thought of them at all.
Yet, when we can find an hour's free time,
We should talk a little more about that business,
If you would grant me the time.

BANQUO Whenever it suits you. 30

MACBETH If you support me, when the hour comes,
It will bring you honor.

BANQUO If I lose none
In seeking to enlarge it, and keep
My conscience free and my allegiance clear, 35
I shall listen to your counsel.

MACBETH Good rest till then!

BANQUO Thanks, sir. The same to you!

Exit BANQUO *and* FLEANCE

MACBETH Go ask your mistress, when my drink is ready,
To strike the bell. And then, go to bed. 40

Exit SERVANT

Is this a dagger which I see before me,
Its handle toward my hand? Come, let me clutch you.
I have you not, and yet I see you still.
Deadly vision, are you not as real
To feeling as to sight? Or are you but 45
A dagger of the mind, a false creation,
Proceeding from my feverish brain?
I see you still, in a form as palpable
As this which now I draw.
You direct me the way that I was going, 50
And the weapon I was to use.

Mine eyes are made the fools of the other senses,

Or else worth all the rest. I see thee still;

And on thy blade and dudgeon gouts of blood,

Which was not so before. There's no such thing.   55

Is it the bloody business which informs

Thus to mine eyes. Now o'er the one half-world

Nature seems dead, and wicked dreams abuse

The curtained sleep. Witchcraft celebrates

Pale Hecate's offerings; and withered murder,   60

Alarmed by his sentinel, the wolf,

Whose howl's his watch, thus with his stealthy pace,

With Tarquin's ravishing strides, towards his design

Moves like a ghost. Thou sure and firm-set earth,

Hear not my steps which way they walk, for fear   65

The very stones prate of my whereabout

And take the present horror from the time,

Which now suits with it. Whiles I threat, he lives;

Words to the heat of deeds too cold breath gives.

A bell rings.

I go, and it is done. The bell invites me.   70

Hear it not, Duncan, for it is a knell

That summons thee to heaven or to hell.

Exit

Scene 2 [*Inverness, Macbeth's castle*]

Enter LADY MACBETH

LADY MACBETH That which hath made them drunk hath made me bold;

What hath quenched them hath given me fire. Hark! Peace!

It was the owl that shrieked, the fatal bellman

Which gives the sternest goodnight. He is about it.

My eyes are made fools by the other senses,
Or else, worth all the rest. I see you still;
And on the blade and handle, spots of blood,
Which were not there before. You don't exist.   55
It is this bloody business that gives this form
To my eyes. Now half the world lies asleep,
Nature seems dead, and wicked dreams abuse
The curtained sleeper. Witches make offerings
To their goddess, pale Hecate, and withered murder,   60
Summoned by his sentinel, the wolf,
Whose howl's his watch, thus with stealthy pace,
With Tarquin's ravishing strides, towards his design
Moves like a ghost. You sure and firm-set earth,
Hear not my steps, the way which I walk, for fear   65
Your very stones tell of my whereabouts
And break the horrified silence,
Which suits me well. While I think threats, he lives;
Words to the heat of deeds a cold breath brings.

A bell rings.

    I go, and it will be done. The bell calls me.   70
Hear it not, Duncan, for it is the knell
That summons you to heaven or to hell.

He exits

Scene 2 [*Macbeth's castle*]

Enter LADY MACBETH

LADY MACBETH That which has made them drunk has made me bold;
    What has quenched them has given me fire. What's that!
    It was the owl that shrieked, a fatal bellman
    That gives the grimmest farewell. He's doing it.

The doors are open, and the surfeited grooms 5
Do mock their charge with snores. I have drugged their possets,
That death and nature do contend about them
Whether they live or die.

MACBETH [*Within*] Who's there? What, ho?

LADY MACBETH Alack, I am afraid they have awaked, 10
And 'tis not done! The attempt, and not the deed,
Confounds us. Hark! I laid their daggers ready;
He could not miss them. Had he not resembled
My father as he slept, I had done it.

Enter MACBETH

My husband! 15

MACBETH I have done the deed. Didst thou not hear a noise?

LADY MACBETH I heard the owl scream and the crickets cry.
Did you not speak?

MACBETH When?

LADY MACBETH Now. 20

MACBETH As I descended?

LADY MACBETH Ay.

MACBETH Hark!
Who lies in the second chamber?

LADY MACBETH Donalbain. 25

MACBETH [*Looking at his hands*] This is a sorry sight.

LADY MACBETH A foolish thought, to say a sorry sight.

MACBETH There's one that did laugh in his sleep, and one cried "Murder!"
That they did wake each other. I stood and heard them.
But they did say their prayers and addressed them 30
Again to sleep.

LADY MACBETH There are two lodged together.

The doors are open, and the drunken officers   5

Do mock their duty with snores. I have drugged their drinks

So that death and nature struggle to decide

Whether they shall live or die.

MACBETH [*Within*] Who's there? What, ho!

LADY MACBETH My God, I am afraid they've awakened,   10

And it's not done! The attempt, and not the deed,

Will ruin us. Hark! I had laid their daggers ready;

He could not miss them. Had Duncan not looked like

My father as he slept, I'd have done the deed myself.

Enter MACBETH

My husband!   15

MACBETH I have done it. Did you not hear a noise?

LADY MACBETH I heard the owls scream and the crickets cry.

Didn't you speak?

MACBETH When?

LADY MACBETH Just now.   20

MACBETH As I came down the stairs?

LADY MACBETH Yes.

MACBETH Listen!

Who lies in the other room?

LADY MACBETH Donalbain.   25

MACBETH [*Looking at his hands*] This is a sorry sight.

LADY MACBETH A foolish thought, to say a sorry sight.

MACBETH One laughed in his sleep, and the other cried "Murder!"

So they did wake each other. I stood and heard them.

But they did say their prayers and prepared   30

Again to sleep.

LADY MACBETH There are two roomed together.

MACBETH One cried "God bless us!" and "Amen!" the other,

As they had seen me with these hangman's hands,

Listening their fear. I could not say "Amen!"   35

When they did say "God bless us!"

LADY MACBETH Consider it not so deeply.

MACBETH But wherefore could not I pronounce "Amen"?

I had most need of blessing, and "Amen"

Stuck in my throat.   40

LADY MACBETH These deeds must not be thought

After these ways. So, it will make us mad.

MACBETH Methought I heard a voice cry "Sleep no more!

Macbeth does murder sleep"—the innocent sleep,

Sleep that knits up the ravelled sleeve of care,   45

The death of each day's life, sore labor's bath,

Balm of hurt minds, great nature's second course,

Chief nourisher in life's feast.

LADY MACBETH What do you mean?

MACBETH Still it cried "Sleep no more!" to all the house;   50

"Glamis hath murdered sleep, and therefore Cawdor

Shall sleep no more! Macbeth shall sleep no more!"

LADY MACBETH Who was it that thus cried? Why, worthy Thane,

You do unbend your noble strength to think

So brainsickly of things. Go get some water   55

And wash this filthy witness from your hand.

Why did you bring these daggers from the place?

They must lie there. Go carry them and smear

The sleepy grooms with blood.

MACBETH I'll go no more.   60

I am afraid to think what I have done;

MACBETH One cried "God bless us!" and the other "Amen,"

As if they had seen me with these bloodstained hands.

Hearing their fear, I could not say "Amen"   35

When they did say "God bless us!"

LADY MACBETH Don't dwell on it.

MACBETH But why could I not say "Amen"?

I had most need of blessing, and "Amen"

Stuck in my throat.   40

LADY MACBETH These deeds must not be pondered

In this way; else, we shall go mad.

MACBETH I thought I heard a voice cry "Sleep no more!

Macbeth has murdered sleep"—innocent sleep,

Sleep that smoothes out the tangled threads of care,   45

The death of each day's life, sore labor's bath,

Balm of hurt minds, great nature's main course,

Chief nourisher at life's feast.

LADY MACBETH What are you talking about?

MACBETH Still it cried "Sleep no more!" to all the house;   50

"Glamis has murdered sleep, and therefore Cawdor

Shall sleep no more; Macbeth shall sleep no more."

LADY MACBETH Who was it that said this? Why, worthy thane,

You undo your noble strength to think

So deliriously of things. Go, get some water   55

And wash the filthy witness from your hand.

Why did you bring these daggers from their place?

They must lie there. Go, carry them, and smear

The sleepy officers with blood.

MACBETH I'll go no more.   60

I am afraid to think what I have done.

Look on it again I dare not.

LADY MACBETH Infirm of purpose!

    Give me the daggers. The sleeping and the dead

    Are but as pictures. 'Tis the eye of childhood

    That fears a painted devil. If he do bleed,   65

    I'll gild the faces of the grooms withal,

    For it must seem their guilt.

                Exit LADY MACBETH *with the daggers*

Knocking within.

MACBETH Whence is that knocking?

    How is it with me when every noise appalls me?   70

    What hands are here? Ha! they pluck out mine eyes!

    Will all great Neptune's ocean wash this blood

    Clean from my hand? No. This my hand will rather

    The multitudinous seas incarnadine,

    Making the green one red.   75

                    Enter LADY MACBETH

LADY MACBETH My hands are of your color, but I shame

    To wear a heart so white. [*Knocking.*] I hear a knocking

    At the south entry. Retire we to our chamber.

    A little water clears us of this deed.

    How easy it is then! Your constancy   80

    Hath left you unattended. [*Knocking.*] Hark, more knocking.

    Get on your nightgown, lest occasion call us

    And show us to be watchers. Be not lost

    So poorly in your thoughts.

MACBETH To know my deed, 'twere best not know myself.   85

    [*Knocking.*] Wake Duncan with thy knocking. I wish thou couldst!

                    Exeunt

Look on it again, I dare not.

LADY MACBETH So weak of purpose!

　　Give me the daggers. The sleeping and the dead

　　Are like pictures. It is the eye of childhood　　　　　　　　65

　　That fears a painted devil. If Duncan still bleeds,

　　I'll smear the faces of his officers with blood,

　　For it must seem their guilt.

　　　　　　　　　　　　Exit LADY MACBETH *with the daggers*

Knocking within.

MACBETH From where does that knocking come?

　　What's wrong with me, when every noise startles?　　　70

　　What hands are here? Ha! they pluck out my eyes!

　　Will all great Neptune's ocean wash this blood

　　Clean from my hand? No, this hand of mine will rather

　　Turn multitudinous seas incarnadine,

　　Making the green one red.　　　　　　　　　　　　　75

　　　　　　　　　　Enter LADY MACBETH

LADY MACBETH My hands are now as red as yours, but I shame

　　To wear a heart so white. [*Knocking.*] I hear a knocking

　　At the south entry. Let us retire to our room.

　　A little water clears us of this deed;

　　How easy it is then. Your firmness of purpose　　　　80

　　Has deserted you. [*Knocking.*] Listen, more knocking.

　　Put on your night robe, lest occasion call

　　And reveal us still awake. Don't be so

　　Lost in your thoughts.

MACBETH To know what I have done, it were best not to know myself. 85

　　[*Knocking.*] Wake Duncan with your knocking. I wish you could.

　　　　　　　　　　　　　　　They exit

Scene 3 [*Macbeth's castle*]

Enter a PORTER, *loud knocking*

PORTER Here's a knocking indeed! If a man were porter of hell gate,
he should have old turning the key. [*Knocking.*] Knock, knock,
knock! Who's there, in the name of Belzebub? Here's a farmer
that hanged himself on the expectation of plenty. Come in time!
Have napkins enow about you; here you'll sweat for it. 5
[*Knocking.*] Knock, knock! Who's there, in the other devil's
name? Faith, here's an equivocator, that could swear in both the
scales against either scale; who committed treason enough for
God's sake, yet could not equivocate to heaven. O, come in,
equivocator! [*Knocking.*] Knock, knock, knock! Who's there? 10
Faith, here's an English tailor come hither for stealing out of
a French hose. Come in tailor. Here you may roast your goose.
[*Knocking.*] Knock, knock! Never at quiet! What are you?
But this place is too cold for hell. I'll devil-porter it no
further. I had thought to have let in some of all professions 15
that go the primrose way to the everlasting bonfire. [*Knocking.*]
Anon, anon! [*Opens the gate.*]

Enter MACDUFF *and* LENNOX

I pray you, remember the porter.

MACDUFF Was it so late, friend, ere you went to bed,
That you do lie so late? 20

PORTER Faith, sir, we were carousing till the second cock; and drink,
sir, is a great provoker of three things.

MACDUFF What three things does drink especially provoke?

PORTER Marry, sir, nose-painting, sleep, and urine. Lechery, sir,
it provokes and unprovokes: it provokes the desire, but it takes 25
away the performance. Therefore, much drink may be said to be
an equivocator with lechery: it makes him, and it mars him;

Scene 3 [*Macbeth's castle*]

Enter a PORTER, *loud knocking*

PORTER   That's knocking, indeed. If a man were porter at the gates
of hell, he should be busy turning the key. [*Knocking.*] Knock,
knock, knock. Who's there, in the name of Beelzebub? Here's
a farmer that hanged himself, expecting his prices to rise. Come
in, time-server, but have plenty of handkerchiefs, for here you'll   5
sweat for sure. [*Knocking.*] Knock, knock. Who's there, in the
other devil's name? Faith, it's the deceiver, who could swear
on either side against the other; who committed treason often for
the sake of God, but could not deceive heaven. O, come in,
deceiver. [*Knocking.*] Knock, knock, knock. Who's there now?   10
Faith, it's an English tailor sent here for stealing material from
French breeches. Come in, tailor, you may heat your iron here.
[*Knocking.*] Knock, knock! Always busy. What are you? This
place is too cold for hell. I'll devil-porter it no more. I had
thought to have let in some of all professions that take the   15
primrose way to the everlasting bonfire. [*Knocking.*] All right,
all right. [*Opens the gate.*]

Enter MACDUFF *and* LENNOX

I pray you, remember to tip the porter.

MACDUFF   Was it so late, friend, when you went to bed
That you have slept so late?   20

PORTER   Faith, sir, we did carouse till after three; and drink, sir, does
provoke three things.

MACDUFF   And what three things does drink especially provoke?

PORTER   Really, sir, rosy noses, sleep, and urine. Lechery, sir, it
provokes and unprovokes: it provokes the desire, but it takes   25
away the performance. Therefore, much drink may be said
to be a deceiver of lechery: it makes him, and it mars him;

it sets him on, and it takes him off; it persuades him,

and disheartens him; makes him stand to, and not stand to;

in conclusion, equivocates him in a sleep, and, giving him the lie,   30

leaves him.

MACDUFF I believe drink gave thee the lie last night

PORTER That it did, sir, in the very throat on me; but I requited him

    for his lie; and, I think, being too strong for him, though he

    took up my legs sometime, yet I made a shift to cast him.   35

MACDUFF Is thy master stirring?

Enter MACBETH

    Our knocking has awaked him; here he comes.

LENNOX Good morrow, noble sir.

MACBETH Good morrow, both.

MACDUFF Is the King stirring, worthy Thane?   40

MACBETH Not yet.

MACDUFF He did command me to call timely on him;

    I have almost slipped the hour.

MACBETH I'll bring you to him.

MACDUFF I know this is a joyful trouble to you;   45

    But yet 'tis one.

MACBETH The labor we delight in physics pain.

    This is the door.

MACDUFF I'll make so bold to call,

    For 'tis my limited service.   50

Exit

LENNOX Goes the King hence today?

MACBETH He does; he did appoint so.

LENNOX The night has been unruly. Where we lay,

    Our chimneys were blown down; and, as they say,

    Lamentings heard in the air, strange screams of death,   55

it sets him on, and it takes him off; it heats him up, and cools
him down; makes him stand to, and not stand to; in conclusion,
drink deceives him with a dream, and, giving him the lie, leaves   30
him flat.

MACDUFF I believe that drink gave you the lie last night.

PORTER That it did, sir, right to my face, but I repaid him for his
lie, and, I think, being too strong for him, though he had me by
the legs at times, yet I contrived to throw him up.   35

MACDUFF Is your master up yet?

Enter MACBETH

Our knocking has awakened him. Here he comes.

LENNOX Good morning, noble sir.

MACBETH Good morning to you both.

MACDUFF Has the King arisen, worthy thane?   40

MACBETH Not yet.

MACDUFF He did command me to call him early.
I almost missed the time.

MACBETH I'll bring you to him.

MACDUFF I know this is a joyful trouble to you,   45
But it is a trouble all the same.

MACBETH The pleasure we take eases any pain.
There is the door.

MACDUFF I'll go right in,
For it is my duty.   50

Exit MACDUFF

LENNOX Does the king leave today?

MACBETH He does; he did arrange it so.

LENNOX Last night was stormy. Where we were,
The chimneys were blown down; and, so they say,
Anguished cries filled the air, strange screams of death,   55

And prophesying, with accents terrible,
Of dire combustion and confused events
New hatched to the woeful time. The obscure bird
Clamored the livelong night. Some say the earth
Was feverous and did shake.   60
MACBETH 'Twas a rough night.
LENNOX My young remembrance cannot parallel
    A fellow to it.

Enter MACDUFF

MACDUFF O horror, horror, horror! Tongue nor heart
    Cannot conceive nor name thee!   65
MACBETH, LENNOX What's the matter?
MACDUFF Confusion now hath made his masterpiece!
    Most sacrilegious murder hath broke ope
    The Lord's anointed temple and stole thence
    The life of the building!   70
MACBETH What is it you say? The life?
LENNOX Mean you his Majesty?
MACDUFF Approach the chamber, and destroy your sight
    With a new Gorgon. Do not bid me speak.
    See, and then speak yourselves   75
                              Exeunt MACBETH *and* LENNOX
    Awake, Awake!
    Ring the alarum bell. Murder and treason!
    Banquo and Donalbain! Malcolm! Awake!
    Shake off this downy sleep, death's counterfeit,
    And look on death itself! Up, up, and see   80
    The great doom's image! Malcolm! Banquo!
    As from your graves, rise up and walk like sprites
    To countenance this horror! Ring the bell!

And prophecies with terrible cries
Of dire destruction and confused events
Newly hatched to the woeful time. The owls
Clamored the livelong night. Some say the earth
Was fevered and did shake.   60
MACBETH   It was a rough night.
LENNOX   In my youthful memory,
    I cannot remember another like it.

                 Enter MACDUFF

MACDUFF   O horrible! It's horrible!
    Neither tongue nor heart can describe it!   65
MACBETH, LENNOX   What's the matter?
MACDUFF   Destruction has now made his masterpiece!
    Most sacrilegious murder has broke open
    The Lord's anointed temple and stole
    Its very life.   70
MACBETH   What is it you're saying—its life?
LENNOX   Do you mean his Majesty?
MACDUFF   Approach his chamber and destroy your sight
    With a new Gorgon. Don't bid me speak;
    Go, see for yourselves.   75

                 Exit MACBETH *and* LENNOX

    Awake, awake!
    Ring the alarm. Murder and treason!
    Banquo and Donalbain! Malcolm, awake!
    Shake off this downy sleep, death's counterfeit,
    And look upon death itself! Up, up, and see   80
    Doomsday's image! Malcolm! Banquo!
    As from your graves, rise up and walk like ghosts
    In keeping with this horror. Ring the bell!

Bell rings. Enter LADY MACBETH

LADY MACBETH What's the business,

    That such a hideous trumpet calls to parley   85

    The sleepers of the house? Speak, speak!

MACDUFF O gentle lady,

    'Tis not for you to hear what I can speak!

    The repetition in a woman's ear

    Would murder as it fell.   90

                Enter BANQUO

    O Banquo, Banquo,

    Our royal master's murdered!

LADY MACBETH Woe, alas!

    What, in our house?

BANQUO Too cruel anywhere.   95

    Dear Duff, I prithee contradict thyself

    And say it is not so.

            Enter MACBETH *and* LENNOX

MACBETH Had I but died an hour before this chance,

    I had lived a blessed time; for from this instant

    There's nothing serious in mortality;   100

    All is but toys; renown and grace is dead;

    The wine of life is drawn, and the mere lees

    Is left this vault to brag of.

          Enter MALCOLM *and* DONALBAIN

DONALBAIN What is amiss?

MACBETH You are, and do not know it.   105

    The spring, the head, the fountain of your blood

    Is stopped, the very source of it is stopped.

Bell rings. Enter LADY MACBETH

LADY MACBETH What's the trouble

That such a hideous noise calls to conference   85

The sleepers in this house? Speak, speak!

MACDUFF O gentle lady,

It's not for you to hear what I might say:

The recital in a woman's ear

Would murder as it fell.   90

Enter BANQUO

O Banquo, Banquo,

Our royal master's murdered!

LADY MACBETH O, no!

What! In our house?

BANQUO Too cruel to happen anywhere.   95

Dear Duff, please contradict yourself,

And say it is not so.

Enter MACBETH *and* LENNOX

MACBETH Had but I died an hour before this great loss,

I'd have lived a happy life, but from this moment on,

There's nothing worth living for;   100

All is but toys. Renown and grace is dead,

The wine of life is drawn, and mere dregs are

Left in the cask to brag of.

Enter MALCOLM *and* DONALBAIN

DONALBAIN What is amiss?

MACBETH You are, and do not know it.   105

The spring, the head, the fountain of your blood,

Is stopped; the very source of it is stopped.

MACDUFF Your royal father's murdered.

MALCOLM O, by whom?

LENNOX Those of his chamber, as it seemed, had done it.   110
    Their hands and faces were all badged with blood;
    So were their daggers, which unwiped we found
    Upon their pillows. They stared and were distracted.
    No man's life was to be trusted with them.

MACBETH O, yet I do repent me of my fury   115
    That I did kill them.

MACDUFF Wherefore did you so?

MACBETH Who can be wise, amazed, temperate and furious,
    Loyal and neutral, in a moment? No man.
    The expedition of my violent love   120
    Outrun the pauser, reason. Here lay Duncan,
    His silver skin laced with his golden blood,
    And his gashed stabs looked like a breach in nature
    For ruin's wasteful entrance; there, the murderers,
    Steeped in the colors of their trade, their daggers   125
    Unmannerly breached with gore. Who could refrain
    That had a heart to love and in that heart
    Courage to make's love known?

LADY MACBETH Help me hence, ho!

MACDUFF Look to the lady.   130

MALCOLM [*Aside to* DONALBAIN] Why do we hold our tongues,
    That most may claim this argument for ours?

DONALBAIN [*Aside to* MALCOLM] What should be spoken here, where
        our fate
    Hid in an auger hole, may rush and seize us? Let's away.   135
    Our tears are not yet brewed.

MALCOLM [*Aside to* DONALBAIN] Nor our strong sorrow

MACDUFF Your royal father's murdered.

MALCOLM What? By whom?

LENNOX His officers, it seems, have done it: 110

   Their hands and faces were all marked with blood;

   So were their daggers which we found unwiped

   Upon their pillows. They stared and acted confused;

   No man's life was to be trusted with them.

MACBETH And yet I do regret my fury,   115

   That I did kill them.

MACDUFF Why did you do such a thing?

MACBETH Who can be wise, bewildered, temperate and furious,

   Loyal and neutral, all at the same time. No man.

   In haste my violent love   120

   Outran my reason. Here lay Duncan,

   His silver skin laced with his golden blood,

   And his gashed stabs looked like a breach in nature

   For ruin's wasteful entrance; there, the murderers,

   Steeped in the colors of their trade, their daggers   125

   Indecently clothed in gore. Who could refrain,

   That had a heart to love, and in that heart,

   Courage to make his love known?

LADY MACBETH O help me. I'm faint.

MACDUFF Look to the lady.   130

MALCOLM [Aside to DONALBAIN] Why do we hold our tongues,

   We that have the most at stake here?

DONALBAIN [Aside to MALCOLM] What should we say here, where
         our fate,

   Hiding in ambush, may rush out and seize us? Let's leave;   135

   Our tears are not yet ready to pour.

MALCOLM [Aside to DONALBAIN] Nor is our strong sorrow

63

Upon the foot of motion.

BANQUO Look to the lady.

> [LADY MACBETH *is helped from the room*]

And when we have our naked frailties hid,   140

That suffer in exposure, let us meet

And question this most bloody piece of work,

To know it further. Fears and scruples shake us.

In the great hand of God I stand, and thence

Against the undivulged pretence I fight   145

Of treasonous malice.

MACDUFF And so do I.

ALL So all.

MACBETH Let's briefly put on manly readiness

And meet in the hall together   150

ALL Well contented.

> [*Exeunt all but* MALCOLM *and* DONALBAIN]

MALCOLM What will you do? Let's not consort with them.

To show an unfelt sorrow is an office

Which the false man does easy. I'll to England.

DONALBAIN To Ireland I. Our separated fortune   155

Shall keep us both the safer. Where we are,

There's daggers in men's smiles; the near in blood,

The nearer bloody.

MALCOLM This murderous shaft that's shot

Hath not yet lighted, and our safest way   160

Is to avoid the aim. Therefore to horse!

And let us not be dainty of leave-taking,

Ready to express itself.

BANQUO Look to the lady.

[LADY MACBETH is helped from the room]

And when we have covered our shivering bodies,   140

That suffer in exposure, let us meet

And examine this most bloody piece of work

To find out what we can. Fears and doubts shake us.

In the great hand of God I stand, and there

I fight against the hidden intentions   145

Of treasonous malice.

MACDUFF And so do I.

ALL So do we all.

MACBETH Let us quickly clothe ourselves properly

And meet in the hall together.   150

ALL Yes, yes.

Exit all but MALCOLM and DONALBAIN

MALCOLM What will you do? Let's not mix with them.

To show an unfelt sorrow is a duty

That the false man does easily. I'll go to England.

DONALBAIN And I to Ireland. Going our separate ways   155

Shall keep us both safer. Where we are,

There's daggers in men's smiles. The closer to the King,

The more likely one is to be murdered.

MALCOLM This murderous arrow that's been shot

Has not yet landed, and our safest way   160

Is to avoid the aim. Therefore, to horse;

And let us not be polite in leave-taking.

But shift away. There's warrant in that theft
Which steals itself when there's no mercy left.

Exeunt

Scene 4 [*Outside Macbeth's castle*]

Enter ROSS *with an* OLD MAN

OLD MAN Threescore and ten I can remember well;
Within the volume of which time I have seen
Hours dreadful and things strange; but this sore night
Hath trifled former knowings.

ROSS Ha, good father,   5
Thou seest the heavens, as troubled with man's act,
Threatens his bloody stage. By the clock 'tis day,
And yet dark night strangles the traveling lamp.
Is it night's predominance, or the day's shame,
That darkness does the face of earth entomb   10
When living light should kiss it?

OLD MAN 'Tis unnatural,
Even like the deed that's done. On Tuesday last
A falcon, towering in her pride of place,
Was by a mousing owl hawked and killed.   15

ROSS And Duncan's horses (a thing most strange and certain),
Beauteous and swift, the minions of their race,
Turned wild in nature, broke their stalls, flung out,
Contending 'gainst obedience, as they would make
War with mankind.   20

OLD MAN 'Tis said they eat each other.

ROSS They did so, to the amazement of mine eyes
That looked upon it.

Enter MACDUFF

Let's slip away. There's justice in that theft

Which takes itself, since there's no mercy here.

They exit

Scene 4 [*Outside Macbeth's castle*]

Enter ROSS *with an* OLD MAN

OLD MAN Seventy years I can remember well,

During which time I have seen

Terrible and strange things, but this sorrowful night

Has made a trifle of them all.

ROSS Ah, good father,   5

Just look at the heavens, so troubled by man's acts,

They threaten his bloody stage. By the clock, it's day,

Yet dark night still strangles our sun.

Is it night's predominance or the day's shame

That darkens the face of earth,   10

When living light should kiss it?

OLD MAN It's unnatural,

Even like the deed that's done. On Tuesday last

A falcon, soaring proudly at the summit of her flight,

Was swooped upon and killed by a mousing owl.   15

ROSS And Duncan's horses—a thing most strange and certain—

Beautiful and swift, the favorites of their breed,

Turned wild in nature, broke their stalls, flung out,

Rebelling against obedience, as if they would make

War with mankind.   20

OLD MAN It's said they ate each other.

ROSS They did so, to the amazement of my eyes

That looked upon it.

Enter MACDUFF

Here comes the good Macduff,

How goes the world, sir, now?   25

MACDUFF Why, see you not?

ROSS Is it known who did this more than bloody deed?

MACDUFF Those that Macbeth hath slain.

ROSS Alas, the day!

What good could they pretend?   30

MACDUFF They were suborned.

Malcolm and Donalbain, the King's two sons,

Are stolen away and fled, which puts upon them

Suspicion of the deed.

ROSS 'Gainst nature still!   35

Thriftless ambition, that wilt raven up

Thine own life's means! Then 'tis most like

The sovereignty will fall upon Macbeth.

MACDUFF He is already named, and gone to Scone

To be invested.   40

ROSS Where is Duncan's body?

MACDUFF Carried to Colmekill,

The sacred storehouse of his predecessors

And guardian of their bones.

ROSS Will you to Scone?   45

MACDUFF No, cousin, I'll to Fife.

ROSS Well, I will thither.

MACDUFF Well, may you see things well done there. Adieu,

Lest our old robes sit easier than our new!

ROSS Farewell, father.   50

OLD MAN God's benison go with you, and with those

That would make good of bad, and friends of foes!

Exeunt omnes

Here comes the good Macduff.

How goes the world now, sir?   25

MACDUFF Why, can't you tell?

ROSS Is it known who did this bloody deed?

MACDUFF Those that Macbeth has slain.

ROSS Alas!

What did they stand to gain?   30

MACDUFF They were bribed.

Malcolm and Donalbain, the King's two sons,

Have stolen away and fled, which places them under

Suspicion of the deed.

ROSS It's against nature: 35

Wasteful ambition that will devour

One's own prospects! Then most likely

The sovereignty will fall upon Macbeth.

MACDUFF He is already named, and gone to Scone

To be crowned king.   40

ROSS Where is Duncan's body?

MACDUFF Carried to Colmekill,

The sacred crypt of his ancestors

And guardian of their bones.

ROSS Will you go to Scone?   45

MACDUFF No, cousin—to Fife, my home.

ROSS Well, I will go to Scone.

MACDUFF Well—you may see things done well there—Adieu!

May Macbeth rule as well as did our Duncan.

ROSS Farewell, old man.   50

OLD MAN God's blessing go with you and with those

Who would make good of bad, and friends of foes.

Exit all

Act Three

Enter BANQUO

BANQUO Thou hast it now—King, Cawdor, Glamis, all,
    As the Weird Women promised; and I fear
    Thou play'dst most foully for it. Yet it was said
    It should not stand in thy posterity,
    But that myself should be the root and father   5
    Of many kings. If there come truth from them,
    (As upon thee, Macbeth, their speeches shine),
    Why, by the verities on thee made good,
    May they not be my oracles as well
    And set me up in hope? But, hush, no more!   10
Sennet sounded.

    Enter MACBETH *as King;* LADY MACBETH *as Queen;* LENNOX,
      ROSS, LORDS, *and* ATTENDANTS

MACBETH Here's our chief guest.

LADY MACBETH If he had been forgotten,
    It had been as a gap in our great feast,
    An all-thing unbecoming.

MACBETH Tonight we hold a solemn supper, sir,   15
    And I'll request your presence.

BANQUO Let your Highness
    Command upon me, to the which my duties
    Are with a most indissoluble tie
    Forever knit.   20

MACBETH Ride you this afternoon?

BANQUO Ay, my good lord.

Act Three

Scene 1 [*Forres. The king's palace*]

Enter BANQUO

BANQUO You have it now—King, Cawdor, Glamis, all,
　　Just as the Weird Sisters promised, and I fear
　　You played most foully for it. Yet they said
　　It should not pass to your descendants,
　　But that I should be the root and father　　　　　　5
　　Of many kings. If there be some truth in them,
　　(As upon you, Macbeth, their speeches shine),
　　Why, by the truths made good to you,
　　May they not be my oracles as well,
　　And set up hope in me? But hush, no more.　　　　10

Trumpet flourish.

　　Enter MACBETH *as King;* LADY MACBETH *as Queen;* LENNOX,
　　　　ROSS, LORDS, *and* ATTENDANTS

MACBETH Here's our chief guest.

LADY MACBETH If he had been forgotten,
　　It would have been a gap in our great feast,
　　Wholly inappropriate.

MACBETH Tonight we hold a state dinner, sir,　　　　15
　　And I'll request your presence.

BANQUO Let your Highness
　　But command me, and my duties
　　Bind me to that command
　　Forever.　　　　　　　　　　　　　　　　　20

MACBETH Are you riding this afternoon?

BANQUO Yes, my good lord.

MACBETH We should have else desired your good advice
    (Which still hath been both grave and prosperous)
    In this day's council; but we'll take tomorrow,   25
    Is it far you ride?

BANQUO As far, my lord, as will fill up the time
    'Twixt this and supper. Go not my horse the better,
    I must become a borrower of the night
    For a dark hour or twain.   30

MACBETH Fail not our feast.

BANQUO My lord, I will not.

MACBETH We hear our bloody cousins are bestowed
    In England and in Ireland, not confessing
    Their cruel parricide, filling their hearers   35
    With strange invention. But of that tomorrow,
    When therewithal we shall have cause of state
    Craving us jointly. Hie you to horse. Adieu,
    Till you return at night. Goes Fleance with you?

BANQUO Ay, my good lord. Our time does call upon's.   40

MACBETH I wish your horses swift and sure of foot.
    And so I do commend you to their backs.
    Farewell.

                               Exit BANQUO

    Let every man be master of his time
    Till seven at night. To make society   45
    The sweeter welcome, we will keep ourself
    Till supper time alone. While then, God be with you!

              Exeunt LORDS. *Manent* MACBETH *and a* SERVANT
    Sirrah, a word with you. Attend those men
    Our pleasure?

SERVANT They are, my lord, without the palace gate.   50

MACBETH We should have otherwise desired your good advice

    (Which has always been both wise and profitable)

    In this day's council; but we'll see you there tomorrow.   25

    Are you riding far?

BANQUO As far, my lord, as will fill up the time

    Between now and supper. Unless my horse is faster than I expect,

    I shall have to continue my ride

    For an hour or two after dark.   30

MACBETH Don't miss our feast.

BANQUO My lord, I will not.

MACBETH We hear our bloody cousins are settled

    In England and in Ireland, not confessing

    Their cruel parricide, but spreading around   35

    Lies and falsehoods. But more of that tomorrow,

    When public affairs shall require both

    Your attention and mine. Hurry to your horse. Adieu,

    Till you return at night. Is Fleance going with you?

BANQUO Yes, my good lord. And we are ready now.   40

MACBETH May your horses be swift and sure of foot,

    And thus I entrust you to their backs.

    Farewell.

Exit BANQUO

    Let every man do as he likes

    Till seven tonight. To make your company   45

    All the sweeter, we will keep to ourself

    Till supper-time. Until then, God be with you.

Exit all except MACBETH *and a* SERVANT

    You there, a word. Are those men

    Still waiting?

SERVANT They are, my lord, outside the palace gate.   50

MACBETH Bring them before us.

Exit SERVANT

To be thus is nothing,
But to be safely thus. Our fears in Banquo
Stick deep; and in his royalty of nature
Reigns that which would be feared. 'Tis much he dares,   55
And to that dauntless temper of his mind
He hath a wisdom that doth guide his valor
To act in safety. There is none but he
Whose being I do fear; and under him
My genius is rebuked, as it is said   60
Mark Antony's was by Caesar. He chid the sisters
When first they put the name of king upon me,
And bade them speak to him. Then, prophet-like,
They hailed him as father to a line of kings.
Upon my head they placed a fruitless crown   65
And put a barren scepter in my grip,
Thence to be wrenched with an unlineal hand,
No son of mine succeeding. If it be so,
For Banquo's issue have I filed my mind;
For them the gracious Duncan have I murdered;   70
Put rancors in the vessel of my peace
Only for them, and mine eternal jewel
Given to the common enemy of man
To make them kings, the seeds of Banquo kings!
Rather than so, come, Fate, into the list,   75
And champion me to the utterance! Who's there?

Enter SERVANT and two MURDERERS

MACBETH Bring them to us.

Exit SERVANT

To be king is nothing,

Unless I am safely king. Our fears of Banquo

Stick deep, and in his nature, there's a

Royalty which should be feared. He has courage,   55

And to that fearless quality of his mind,

He has a wisdom that does guide his valor

To act in sure ways. There is none but he

Whose being I do fear; and under him

My spirit is cowed, as it is said   60

Mark Antony's was by Caesar. He scolded the hags

When they first put the name of king upon me

And told them to speak to him. Then, prophet-like,

They hailed him father to a line of kings.

Upon my head, they placed a fruitless crown   65

And put a barren scepter in my grasp,

To be wrenched by a hand not of my line,

No son of mine succeeding. If true, then

For Banquo's offspring I've corrupted my mind,

For them the gracious Duncan I have murdered,   70

Put poison in the vessel of my peace

Only for them, and my immortal soul

Given to Satan, the enemy of man,

To make them kings, the seed of Banquo kings!

Rather than that, I'll war with fate itself   75

And fight to the death. Who's there?

Reenter SERVANT *with two* MURDERERS

Now go to the door and stay there till we call.

Exit SERVANT

Was it not yesterday we spoke together?

MURDERERS It was, so please your Highness.

MACBETH Well then, now   80

Have you considered of my speeches? Know

That it was he, in the times past, which held you

So under fortune, which you thought had been

Our innocent self. This I made good to you

In our last conference, passed in probation with you   85

How you were borne in hand, how crossed; the instruments;

Who wrought with them; and all things else that might

To half a soul and to a notion crazed

Say "Thus did Banquo."

FIRST MURDERER You made it known to us.   90

MACBETH I did so; and went further, which is now

Our point of second meeting. Do you find

Your patience so predominant in your nature

That you can let this go? Are you so gospelled

To pray for this good man and for his issue,   95

Whose heavy hand hath bowed you to the grave

And beggared your forever?

FIRST MURDERER We are men, my liege.

MACBETH Ay, in the catalogue ye go for men,

As hounds and greyhounds, mongrels, spaniels, curs,   100

Shoughs, water-rugs, and demi-wolves are clept

All by the name of dogs. The valued file

Distinguishes the swift, the slow, the subtle,

The housekeeper, the hunter, every one

According to the gift which bounteous nature   105

Now go to the door, and stay there till we call.

Exit SERVANT

Was it not yesterday we spoke together?

MURDERERS It was, so please your Highness.

MACBETH Well then, now   80

Have you thought over what I said? You know

That it was Banquo who, in times past, kept you

From knowing any success, which you had thought was

Our innocent self. This I proved to you

In our last conference, showing you the evidence of how   85

You were led up the garden path, how thwarted; the means;

Who made them; and all other things that might

To even a half-wit or a crazed mind

Say, "This did Banquo."

FIRST MURDERER You made it known to us.   90

MACBETH I did so; and went further, which is now

The point of our second meeting. Do you find

Patience so dominate in your nature

That you can let this go? Are you so soaked in Gospel

That you can pray for this man, and for his offspring,   95

Whose heavy hand has made sure you'll die poor

And beggared your children forever?

FIRST MURDERER We are men, your liege.

MACBETH Yes, in a mere listing, you pass for men,

Much the same as hounds and greyhounds, mongrels, spaniels, curs,   100

Lap dogs, retrievers, and half-wolves all are called

By the name of dog. A more valued way

Distinguishes the swift, the slow, the subtle,

The watchdog, the hunter, every one

According the gift that bounteous nature   105

Hath in him closed; whereby he does receive

Particular addition, from the bill

That writes them all alike; and so of men.

Now, if you have a station in the file,

Not in the worst rank of manhood, say it; 110

And I will put that business in your bosoms

Whose execution takes your enemy off,

Grapples you to the heart and love of us,

Who wear our health but sickly in his life,

Which in his death were perfect. 115

SECOND MURDERER I am one, my liege,

Whom the vile blows and buffets of the world

Hath so incensed that I am reckless what

I do to spite the world.

FIRST MURDERER And I another, 120

So weary with disasters, tugged with fortune,

That I would set my life on any chance,

To mend it or be rid on it.

MACBETH Both of you

Know Banquo was your enemy. 125

MURDERERS True, my lord.

MACBETH So he is mine; and in such bloody distance

That every minute of his being thrusts

Against my nearest of life; and though I could

With barefaced power sweep him from my sight 130

And bid my will avouch it, yet I must not,

For certain friends that are both his and mine,

Whose loves I may not drop, but wail his fall

Who I myself struck down. And thence it is

Has given to him, whereby he does receive

Distinction from the general list

That writes them all alike; so, too, of men.

Now, if you have a place in the general list of men

That's not in the lowest rank of manhood, say so,   110

And then I'll put in your secret care a project

Whose execution takes your enemy off,

And binds you close to our heart and love.

We wear our health uncertainly so long as he lives,

But it would be perfect in his death.   115

SECOND MURDERER I am one, my liege,

Whom the vile blows and buffets of the world

Have so incensed that I am reckless what

I do to spite the world.

FIRST MURDERER And I another,   120

So weary with disasters, dragged about by fortune,

That I would gladly risk my life

To mend it or be rid of it.

MACBETH Both of you

Know that Banquo's your enemy.   125

MURDERERS True, my lord.

MACBETH So is he mine, and so dangerously close

That every minute he lives thrusts

Against my very heart. And though I could

With barefaced power sweep him from my sight   130

And justify it by my will alone, yet I must not,

Because of friends that are both his and mine,

Whose loyalty I dare not lose, but, instead, bewail his death

When I myself did cause it. And so it is

That I to your assistance do make love,   135

Masking this business from the common eye

For sundry weighty reasons.

SECOND MURDERER We shall, my lord,

Perform what you command us.

FIRST MURDERER Though our lives—   140

MACBETH Your spirits shine through you. Within this hour at most

I will advise you where to plant yourselves,

Acquaint you with the perfect spy of the time,

The moment on it; for it must be done tonight,

And something from the palace; always thought   145

That I require a clearness; and with him,

To leave no rubs nor blotches in the work,

Fleance his son, that keeps him company,

Whose absence is no less material to me

Than is his father's, must embrace the fate   150

Of that dark hour. Resolve yourselves apart;

I'll come to you anon.

MURDERERS We are resolved, my lord.

MACBETH I'll call upon you straight. Abide within.

Exeunt MURDERERS

It is concluded. Banquo, thy soul's flight,   155

If it find heaven, must find it tonight.

Exit MACBETH

Scene 2 [*Forres. The king's palace*]

Enter LADY MACBETH *and a* SERVANT

LADY MACBETH Is Banquo gone from court?

SERVANT Ay, madam, but returns again tonight.

That I do court your help,   135

Masking the business from the public's eye

For various weighty reasons.

SECOND MURDERER We shall, my lord,

Perform what you command us.

FIRST MURDERER Though our lives—   140

MACBETH Your courage is evident. Within this hour at most,

I will advise you where to plant yourselves,

Acquaint you with the exact hour of the time,

The moment for it, for the deed must be done tonight,

And somewhat away from the palace; bear in mind   145

That I must be kept clear of it—and with him,

To leave no roughness nor botches in the work,

And Fleance his son who accompanies him,

Whose death is no less important to me

Than his father's, must embrace the fate   150

Of that dark hour. Make up your minds in private,

I'll come to you soon.

MURDERERS We are resolved, my lord.

MACBETH I'll call you straight away; wait inside.

Exit MURDERERS

It is settled. Banquo, your soul's flight,   155

If it find heaven, must find it out tonight.

Exit MACBETH

Scene 2 [*Forres. The king's palace*]

Enter LADY MACBETH *and a* SERVANT

LADY MACBETH Is Banquo gone from court?

SERVANT Yes, madam, but returns again tonight.

LADY MACBETH Say to the King I would attend his leisure
    For a few words.
SERVANT Madam, I will.   5

                               Exit

LADY MACBETH Naught's had, all's spent,
    Where our desire is got without content.
    'Tis safer to be that which we destroy
    Than by destruction dwell in doubtful joy.

                  Enter MACBETH

    How now, my lord? Why do you keep alone,   10
    Of sorriest fancies your companions making,
    Using those thoughts which should indeed have died
    With them they think on? Things without all remedy
    Should be without regard. What's done is done.
MACBETH We have scorched the snake, not killed it.   15
    She'll close, and be herself, whilst our poor malice
    Remains in danger of her former tooth.
    But let the frame of things disjoint, both the worlds suffer,
    Ere we will eat our meal in fear and sleep
    In the affliction of these terrible dreams   20
    That shake us nightly. Better be with the dead,
    Whom we, to gain our peace, have sent to peace,
    Than on the torture of the mind to lie
    In restless ecstasy. Duncan is in his grave;
    After life's fitful fever, he sleeps well.   25
    Treason has done his worst. Nor steel nor poison,
    Malice domestic, foreign levy, nothing
    Can touch him further.

LADY MACBETH Go tell the King that I wish to have
    A few words with him.
SERVANT Madam, I will.   5

Exit SERVANT

LADY MACBETH Nothing's gained, all's spent,
    When we get what we desire without content.
    It's safer to be that which we destroy
    Than by destruction dwell in doubtful joy.

Enter MACBETH

    How now, my lord? Why do you keep to yourself   10
    Making miserable fancies your companion,
    Which should have died
    When their victims did? Things that cannot be changed
    Should be ignored; what's done is done.
MACBETH We have wounded the snake, not killed it;   15
    She'll heal and be herself while our weak hostility
    Remains in danger of her power to bite.
    Yet let the universe collapse, both heaven and earth perish,
    Before we eat our meal in fear and sleep
    In the affliction of these terrible dreams   20
    That shake us nightly. Better to be with the dead,
    Whom we, to gain our peace, have sent to peace,
    Than on the torture rack of the mind to lie
    In restless frenzy. Duncan is in his grave;
    After life's fitful fever, he sleeps well.   25
    Treason has done its worst. Neither steel nor poison,
    Civil war nor invasion, nothing,
    Can touch him further.

LADY MACBETH Come on.

    Gentle my lord, 30

    Sleek over your rugged looks; be bright and jovial

    Among your guests tonight.

MACBETH So shall I, love; and so, I pray, be you.

    Let your remembrance apply to Banquo;

    Present him eminence both with eye and tongue— 35

    Unsafe the while, that we

    Must lave our honors in these flattering streams

    And make our faces vizards to our hearts,

    Disguising what they are.

LADY MACBETH You must leave this. 40

MACBETH O, full of scorpions is my mind, dear wife!

    Thou knowest that Banquo, and his Fleance, lives.

LADY MACBETH But in them Nature's copy's not eterne.

MACBETH There's comfort yet! They are assailable.

    Then thou be jocund. Ere the bat hath flown 45

    His cloistered flight, ere to black Hecate's summons

    The shard-borne beetle with his drowsy hums

    Hath rung night's yawning peal, there shall be done

    A deed of dreadful note.

LADY MACBETH What's to be done? 50

MACBETH Be innocent of the knowledge, dearest chuck,

    Till thou applaud the deed. Come, sealing night,

    Scarf up the tender eye of pitiful day,

    And with they bloody and invisible hand

    Cancel and tear to pieces that great bond 55

    Which keeps me pale! Light thickens, and the crow

    Makes wing to the rooky wood.

LADY MACBETH Come on.

My noble lord,   30

Smooth over your furrowed brows. Be bright and jovial

Among your guests tonight.

MACBETH So shall I, love; and so, I pray, be you.

Remember to give special attention to Banquo,

Honor him with looks and words—   35

We're still not safe, and we

Must wash our honors in streams of flattery,

And make our faces mask our hearts,

Disguising what is in them.

LADY MACBETH You must stop thinking like this.   40

MACBETH O, full of scorpions is my mind, dear wife!

You know that Banquo and his Fleance live.

LADY MACBETH But they have not been granted eternal life.

MACBETH There's comfort yet; they are vulnerable.

So be you joyful. Before the bat has flown   45

His secluded flight, before the scaly-winged beetle

Answers black Hecate's summons with his drowsy hums

And rings the curfew bell, there shall be done

A deed of dreadful note.

LADY MACBETH What's to be done?   50

MACBETH Be innocent of the knowledge, my dear pet,

Until you can applaud the deed. Come, dark night,

Cover the tender eye of day;

And with your bloody and invisible hand

Cancel and tear to pieces that contract   55

Which keeps me from doing. The light dims, and the crow

Flies off to the rooky wood.

Good things of day begin to droop and drowse,

Whiles night's black agents to their preys do rouse.

Thou marvellest at my words; but hold thee still: 60

Things bad begun make strong themselves by ill.

So prithee go with me.

Exeunt

Scene 3   [*Forres. A park near the palace*]

Enter three MURDERERS

FIRST MURDERER   But who did bid thee join with us?

THIRD MURDERER   Macbeth.

SECOND MURDERER   He needs not our mistrust, since he delivers

Our offices, and what we have to do,

To the direction just.   5

FIRST MURDERER   Then stand with us.

The west yet glimmers with some streaks of day.

Now spurs the lated traveler apace

To gain the timely inn, and near approaches

The subject of our watch.   10

THIRD MURDERER   Hark! I hear horses.

BANQUO [*Within*] Give us a light there, ho!

SECOND MURDERER   Then 'tis he! The rest

That are within the note of expectation

Already are in the court.   15

FIRST MURDERER   His horses go about.

THIRD MURDERER   Almost a mile; but he does usually,

So all men do, from hence to the palace gate

Make it their walk.

Enter BANQUO *and* FLEANCE *with a torch*

SECOND MURDERER   A light, a light!   20

Good things of day begin to droop and drowse,

While night's black agents to their preys do rouse.

You wonder at my words, but just be patient,   60

Evil deeds need more evil to strengthen them.

So, please, just go along with me.

Exit

Scene 3 [*Forres. A park near the palace*]

Enter three MURDERERS

FIRST MURDERER   But who asked you to join with us?

THIRD MURDERER   Macbeth.

SECOND MURDERER   Do not distrust him, since he tells us

Our duties, and what we have to do,

Just as Macbeth directed.   5

FIRST MURDERER   Then stand with us.

The west yet glimmers with some streaks of day;

And spurs the belated traveler

To reach an inn before dark, and nearby the man

We are watching for approaches.   10

THIRD MURDERER   Listen, I hear horses.

BANQUO [*Offstage*]   Give us a light there, ho!

SECOND MURDERER   There's our man. The rest

Of the expected guests

Already are in the court.   15

FIRST MURDERER   His horses seem to wander.

THIRD MURDERER   It's almost a mile to the palace gate,

But he does as most men,

Walk from here.

Enter BANQUO *and* FLEANCE *with a torch*

SECOND MURDERER   A light, a light!   20

THIRD MURDERER 'Tis he.

FIRST MURDERER Stand to it.

BANQUO It will rain tonight.

FIRST MURDERER Let it come down!

[*The three* MURDERERS *attack* BANQUO *and* FLEANCE]

BANQUO O, treachery! Fly, good Fleance, fly, fly, fly!   25

    Thou mayest revenge. O slave! [*He dies.* FLEANCE *escapes*]

THIRD MURDERER Who did strike out the light?

FIRST MURDERER Was't not the way?

THIRD MURDERER There's but one down; the son is fled.

SECOND MURDERER We have lost   30

    Best half of our affair.

FIRST MURDERER Well, let's away, and say how much is done.

                                  Exeunt

Scene 4 [*Forres. Hall in the palace*]

    Banquet prepared. Enter MACBETH, LADY MACBETH, ROSS, LENNOX,

        and ATTENDANTS

MACBETH You know your own degrees, sit down. At first

    And last the hearty welcome.

LORDS Thanks to your Majesty.

MACBETH Ourself will mingle with society

    And play the humble host.   5

    Our hostess keeps her state, but in best time

    We will require her welcome.

LADY MACBETH Pronounce it for me, sir, to all our friends,

    For my heart speaks they are welcome.

              Enter FIRST MURDERER *to the door*

MACBETH See, they encounter thee with their hearts' thanks.   10

    Both sides are even. Here I'll sit in the midst.

    Be large in mirth; anon we'll drink a measure

THIRD MURDERER 'Tis he.

FIRST MURDERER Stand ready.

BANQUO It will be a rainy night.

FIRST MURDERER Let it pour.

[*The three* MURDERERS *attack* BANQUO *and* FLEANCE]

BANQUO O treachery! Fly, good Fleance, fly, fly, fly!   25

    Avenge this deed! O slave! [*He dies.* FLEANCE *escapes*]

THIRD MURDERER Who struck out the light?

FIRST MURDERER Wasn't that right?

THIRD MURDERER There's but one down; the son has fled.

SECOND MURDERER We have lost the most important part.   30

FIRST MURDERER Well, let's get away and report what's done.

                          They exit

Scene 4 [*Forres. Hall in the palace*]

    Banquet prepared. Enter MACBETH, LADY MACBETH, ROSS, LENNOX,

        and ATTENDANTS

MACBETH You all know your rank; sit down. To the first

    as well as the last, a hearty welcome.

LORDS Thanks to your Majesty.

MACBETH We will mingle with the company,

    And play the genial tavern-keeper.   5

    Our hostess will keep to her throne, but at the right time

    We will request her to welcome you.

LADY MACBETH Say it for me, sir, to all our friends,

    For my heart speaks they are welcome.

            Enter FIRST MURDERER *to the door*

MACBETH See, they greet you with their hearts' thanks.   10

    Both sides of the table are equal, so I'll sit here in the middle.

    Be large in mirth; soon I'll drink a toast to

The table round. [*Goes to the door*]

There's blood upon thy face.

FIRST MURDERER 'Tis Banquo's then.   15

MACBETH 'Tis better thee without than he within.

    Is he dispatched?

FIRST MURDERER My lord, his throat is cut. That I did for him.

MACBETH Thou art the best of the cutthroats! Yet he's good

    That did the like for Fleance. If thou didst it,   20

    Thou are the nonpareil.

FIRST MURDERER Most royal sir, Fleance is scaped.

MACBETH [*Aside*] Then comes my fit again. I had else been perfect;

    Whole as the marble, founded as the rock,

    As broad and general as the casing air.   25

    But now I am cabined, cribbed, confined, bound in

    To saucy doubts and fears.—But Banquo's safe?

FIRST MURDERER Ay, my good lord. Safe in the ditch he bides,

    With twenty trenched gashes on his head,

    The least a death to nature.   30

MACBETH Thanks for that!

    There the grown serpent lies; the worm that's fled

    Hath nature that in time will venom breed.

    No teeth for the present. Get thee gone. Tomorrow

    We'll hear ourselves again.   35

                          Exit FIRST MURDERER

LADY MACBETH My royal lord,

    You do not give the cheer. The feast is sold

    That is not often vouched, while 'tis a-making,

    'Tis given with welcome. To feed were best at home

    From thence, the sauce to meat is ceremony;   40

    Meeting were bare without it.

The whole company. [*Goes to the door*]

There's blood on your face.

FIRST MURDERER Then it's Banquo's.   15

MACBETH It's better the blood be on you than within him.

Is he dead then?

FIRST MURDERER My lord, his throat is cut; that I did myself.

MACBETH You are the prince of cutthroats,

Yet he's also good that did the same for Fleance.   20

If you did that, you are a king.

FIRST MURDERER Most royal sir, Fleance has escaped.

MACBETH [*Aside*] Now comes my dread again. Till this I felt fine;

Solid as marble; firm as rock,

As free as the enclosing air;   25

But again I am cabined, cribbed, confined, bound in

Alone with doubts and fears.—But Banquo's dead?

FIRST MURDERER Yes, my good lord. Safe in a ditch he lies,

With twenty deep-cut gashes on his head,

Any one enough to kill a normal man.   30

MACBETH Thanks for that.

There the grown serpent lies; the worm that's fled

Has a nature that in time will venom breed,

But for the present, no teeth. Be gone. Tomorrow,

We shall speak again.   35

          Exit FIRST MURDERER

LADY MACBETH My royal lord,

You are not hospitable. The feast

That is not supported by welcomes, while it takes place,

Is no better than a bought meal. It were better to eat at home.

Elsewhere, the sauce to meat is ceremony;   40

Meeting were bare without it.

MACBETH Sweet remembrancer!

Now good digestion wait on appetite,

And health on both!

LENNOX May it please your Highness sit.   45

MACBETH Here had we now our country's honor, roofed,

Were the graced person of our Banquo present;

The GHOST *of* BANQUO *enters, and sits in* MACBETH'S *place*

Who may I rather challenge for unkindness

Than pity for mischance!

ROSS His absence, sir,   50

Lays blame upon his promise. Please it your Highness

To grace us with your royal company?

MACBETH The table's full.

LENNOX Here is a place reserved, sir.

MACBETH Where?   55

LENNOX Here, my good lord. What is it that moves your Highness?

MACBETH Which of you have done this?

LORDS What, my good lord?

MACBETH [*To the* GHOST] Thou canst not say I did it. Never shake

Thy gory locks at me.   60

ROSS Gentlemen, rise. His Highness is not well.

LADY MACBETH Sit, worthy friends. My lord is often thus,

And hath been from his youth. Pray you keep seat.

The fit is momentary; upon a thought

He will again be well. If you much note him,   65

You shall offend him and extend his passion.

Feed, and regard him not. [*To* MACBETH] Are you a man?

MACBETH Ay, and a bold one, that dare look on that

Which might appall the devil.

MACBETH Sweet reminder!

    Now good digestion go with appetite.

    And health on both.

LENNOX May it please your Highness now to take his seat.   45

MACBETH Here under one roof all our country's nobility,

    Were the graced person of Banquo present;

        The GHOST *of* BANQUO *enters and sits in* MACBETH'S *place*

    Whom I'd rather charge for discourtesy

    Than pity if some accident has befallen him.

ROSS His absence, sir,   50

    Does rebuke his promise. Please it your Highness

    To grace us with your royal company?

MACBETH The table's full.

LENNOX Here is a place reserved, sir.

MACBETH Where?   55

LENNOX Here, my good lord. What is it that bothers your Highness?

MACBETH Which of you has done this?

LORDS Done what, my lord?

MACBETH [*To the* GHOST] You can't say I did it; don't shake

    Your gory locks at me.   60

ROSS Gentlemen, rise; his Highness is not well.

LADY MACBETH Sit, worthy friends. My lord is often thus,

    And has been since his youth. Please, keep your seats;

    The fit is momentary; before you can think it,

    He will again be well. If you take notice,   65

    You shall offend him and prolong his agitation.

    Eat, and regard him not. [*To* MACBETH] Are you a man?

MACBETH Yes, and a bold one, that dares look on that

    Which might appall the devil.

LADY MACBETH O proper stuff! 70

This is the very painting of your fear.

This is the air-drawn dagger which you said

Led you to Duncan. O, these flaws and starts

(Impostors to true fear) would well become

A woman's story at a winter's fire, 75

Authorized by her grandam. Shame itself!

Why do you make such faces? When all's done,

You look but on a stool.

MACBETH Prithee see there! Behold! Look! [*To the* GHOST] Lo!

How say you? 80

Why, what care I? If thou canst nod, speak too,

If charnel houses and our graves must send

Those that we bury back, our monuments

Shall be the maws of kites.

Exit GHOST

LADY MACBETH What, quite unmanned in folly? 85

MACBETH If I stand here, I saw him.

LADY MACBETH Fie, for shame!

MACBETH Blood hath been shed ere now, in the olden time,

Ere humane statute purged the gentle weal;

Ay, and since too, murders have been performed 90

Too terrible for the ear. The time has been

That, when the brains were out, the man would die,

And there an end! But now they rise again,

With twenty mortal murders on their crowns,

And push us from our stools. This is more strange 95

Than such a murder is.

LADY MACBETH My worthy lord,

LADY MACBETH   What nonsense!   70

    This is truly the image of your fear.

    It is like the air-drawn dagger you said

    Led you to Duncan. O, these outbursts

    (Not worthy to be called true fear) sound like

    A young woman's story told at the crackling hearth,   75

    Authored by her grandma. Shame!

    Why do you make such faces? When all's done,

    You look upon an empty seat.

MACBETH   I beg you, look there! Behold, look! [*To the* GHOST] Lo,

    What are you saying?   80

    Why, what do I care? If you can nod, speak too.

    If the vaults of the dead and our graves can send

    Those that we bury back, our tombs

    Shall be the bellies of vultures.

                               Exit GHOST

LADY MACBETH   What, are you unmanned by this folly?   85

MACBETH   As I stood here, I saw him.

LADY MACBETH   Fie, for shame!

MACBETH   Blood has been shed before now, in the old days,

    Before civilizing law cleansed society;

    Yes, and since then too, murders have been performed   90

    Too terrible to speak of. But the time was then

    That, when the brains were out, the man would die,

    And there was an end! But now they rise again,

    With twenty deadly wounds on their head,

    And push us from our place. This is more strange   95

    Than even the murder of Banquo.

LADY MACBETH   My worthy lord,

Your noble friends do lack you.

MACBETH   I do forget.

Do not muse at me, my most worthy friends.   100
I have a strange infirmity, which is nothing
To those that know me. Come, love and health to all!
Then I'll sit down. Give me some wine, fill full.
I drink to the general joy of the whole table,
And to our dear friend Banquo, whom we miss.   105

Enter GHOST

Would he were here! To all, and him, we thirst,
And all to all.

LORDS   Our duties, and the pledge.

MACBETH   Avaunt, and quit my sight! Let the earth hide thee!
Thy bones are marrowless, they blood is cold;   110
Thou hast no speculation in those eyes
Which thou dost glare with!

LADY MACBETH   Think of this, good peers,
But as a thing of custom. 'Tis no other.
Only it spoils the pleasure of the time.   115

MACBETH   What man dare, I dare.
Approach thou like the rugged Russian bear,
The armed rhinoceros, or the Hyrcan tiger;
Take any shape but that, and my firm nerves
Shall never tremble. Or be alive again   120
And dare me to the desert with thy sword.
If trembling I inhabit then, protest me
The baby of a girl. Hence, horrible shadow!
Unreal mockery, hence!

Exit GHOST

Your noble friends miss your company.

MACBETH I did forget.

    Do not wonder at me, my most worthy friends;   100

    I have an odd infirmity, which is nothing

    To those that know me. Come, love and health to all;

    Then I'll sit down. Give me some wine, and fill it full.

    I drink to the general joy of the whole table,

    And to our dear friend Banquo, whom we miss;   105

Enter GHOST

    Would he were here! To all, and him, we drink,

    And all for all.

LORDS We pledge our honor and our loyalty.

MACBETH [*To the* GHOST] Leave, and quit my sight! Let the earth hide you.

    Your bones are marrowless, your blood is cold;   110

    You have no sight in those eyes,

    With which you glare.

LADY MACBETH Think of this, good peers,

    But as a normal occurrence; it's nothing else.

    Yet it spoils the pleasure of the moment.   115

MACBETH What a man will dare, I dare.

    Come at me like the rugged Russian bear,

    The armed rhinoceros, or like the Hyrcan tiger,

    Take any shape but this, and my firm nerves

    Shall never tremble. Or be alive again,   120

    And dare me to single combat with your sword;

    If I tremble then, call me

    A baby, a girl. Begone, horrible shadow!

    Imagined mockery, begone!

Exit GHOST

Why so! Being gone, 125

I am a man again. [*To the* LORDS] Pray you sit still.

LADY MACBETH You have displaced the mirth, broke the good meeting

With most admired disorder.

MACBETH Can such things be,

And overcome us like a summer's cloud 130

Without our special wonder? You make me strange

Even to the disposition that I owe,

When now I think you can behold such sights

And keep the natural ruby of your cheeks

When mine is blanched with fear. 135

ROSS What sights, my lord?

LADY MACBETH I pray you speak not. He grows worse and worse;

Question enrages him. At once, good night.

Stand not on the order of your going,

But go at once. 140

LENNOX Good night, and better health

Attend his Majesty!

LADY MACBETH A kind good night to all!

Exit all but MACBETH *and* LADY MACBETH

MACBETH It will have blood, they say; blood will have blood.

Stones have been known to move and trees to speak; 145

Augures and understood relations have

By maggot-pies and choughs and rooks brought forth

The secretest man of blood. What is the night?

LADY MACBETH Almost at odds with morning, which is which.

MACBETH How sayest thou that Macduff denies his person 150

At our great bidding?

LADY MACBETH Did you send to him, sir?

So, there. It's gone, and 125
I'm my own man again. [*To the* LORDS] Please, sit still.

LADY MACBETH You have driven away the mirth, broken the mood,
With your alarming behavior.

MACBETH Can such things be,
And pass over like a summer's cloud, 130
Causing no surprise? You make me feel
That I do not know my own nature,
When now I see you behold such sights
And keep the natural redness of your cheeks,
When mine turn white with fear. 135

ROSS What sights, my lord?

LADY MACBETH I pray you, speak not. He grows worse and worse;
More talk only upsets him. At once, good night.
Don't bother about the proper leave-taking,
But go, all of you. 140

LENNOX Good night, and better health
Attend his Majesty.

LADY MACBETH A kind good night to all.

> *Exit all but* MACBETH and LADY MACBETH

MACBETH Murder will be avenged, they say. Blood will have blood.
Stones have been known to move and trees to speak; 145
Predictions and hidden relations have
By magpies and crows and rooks revealed
The most secret murderer. What time of night is it?

LADY MACBETH Almost morning. It's hard to say.

MACBETH What do you say to this, that Macduff refuses to come 150
Despite our strong request?

LADY MACBETH Did you send for him, sir?

MACBETH   I hear it by the way; but I will send.

    There's not a one of them but in his house

    I keep a servant feed. I will tomorrow   155

    (And betimes I will) unto the Weird Sisters.

    More shall they speak, for now I am bent to know

    By the worst means the worst. For mine own good

    All causes shall give way. I am in blood

    Stepped in so far that, should I wade no more,   160

    Returning were as tedious as go over.

    Strange things I have in head, that will to hand,

    Which must be acted ere they may be scanned.

LADY MACBETH   You lack the season of all natures, sleep.

MACBETH   Come, we'll to sleep. My strange and self-abuse   165

    Is the initiate fear that wants hard use.

    We are but young in deed.

Exeunt

Scene 5   [*A heath*]

Thunder. Enter the three WITCHES, *meeting* HECATE

FIRST WITCH   Why, how now, Hecate? You look angerly.

HECATE   Have I not reason, beldams as you are,

    Saucy and overbold? How did you dare

    To trade and traffic with Macbeth

    In riddles and affairs of death;   5

    And I, the mistress of your charms,

    The close contriver of all harms,

    Was never called to bear my part

    Or show the glory of our art?

    And, which is worse, all you have done   10

MACBETH I hear it roundabout; but I will send.

    There's not one of them in his house

    Who is not my paid spy. I will go tomorrow   155

    Early to see the Weird Sisters.

    More they shall tell, for now I am determined to know

    By the worst means the worst that can befall. For my own good,

    Everything shall give way. I am so steeped

    In blood that, should I wade no more,   160

    Returning is as difficult as going over to the other side.

    I have in mind some outrageous deeds,

    Which must be acted before they are examined.

LADY MACBETH You lack the preservative of nature, sleep.

MACBETH Come, we'll to sleep. My strange delusion   165

    Is only the beginner's fear that needs more practice.

    We are still novices.

                    MACBETH *and* LADY MACBETH *exit*

Scene 5 [*A heath*]

Thunder. Enter the three WITCHES, *meeting* HECATE

FIRST WITCH Why, how now, Hecate? You seem angry.

HECATE Have I not reason, old hags that you are,

    Insolent and bold? How could you dare

    Trade and traffic with Macbeth

    In riddles and affairs of death;   5

    While I, the mistress of your charms,

    The secret contriver of all harms,

    Was never called to play my part,

    Or show the glory of our art?

    And, what is worse, all you have done   10

Hath been but for a wayward son,

Spiteful and wrathful, who, as others do,

Loves for his own ends, not for you.

But make amends now. Get you gone

And at the pit of Acheron 15

Meet me in the morning. Thither he

Will come to know his destiny.

Your vessels and your spells provide,

Your charms and everything beside.

I am for the air. This night I'll spend 20

Unto a dismal and a fatal end.

Great business must be wrought ere noon.

Upon the corner of the moon

There hangs a vaporous drop profound,

I'll catch it ere it come to ground; 25

And that, distilled by magic sleights,

Shall raise such artificial sprites

As by the strength of their illusion

Shall draw him on to his confusion.

He shall spurn fate, scorn death, and bear 30

His hopes 'bove wisdom, grace, and fear;

And you all know security

Is mortals' chiefest enemy.

Music and song offstage, "Come away, come away," *etc.*

Hark! I am called. My little spirit, see,

Sits in a foggy cloud and stays for me. 35

Exit HECATE

FIRST WITCH Come, let's make haste. She'll soon be back again.

Exeunt

Has been but for a wayward son,

Spiteful and wrathful, who, as others do,

Loves for his own ends, not for you.

But make amends now. Get you gone,

And at the pit of Acheron   15

Meet me in the morning. There he

Will come to know his destiny.

Your vessels and your spells provide,

Your charms, and everything beside.

As for me, this night I'll spend   20

Riding on air, planning his fatal end.

Much must be done before the noon:

Upon the corner of the moon,

There hangs a drop of vapor round

That I'll catch before it hits the ground;   25

And that, distilled by secret rites,

Shall raise deceitful sprites,

Which by the strength of their illusion,

Shall draw him on to his confusion.

He shall spurn fate, scorn death, and bear   30

His hopes above wisdom, grace, and fear;

And, as you know, a false sense of security

Is mortals' chiefest enemy.

Music and a song offstage, "Come away, Come away," *etc.*

Hark! I am called; my little spirit, see,

Sits on a foggy cloud, and waits for me.   35

Exit HECATE

FIRST WITCH Come, let's make haste. She'll soon be back again.

Exit WITCHES

Scene 6 [*Forres. The palace*]

Enter LENNOX and a LORD

LENNOX My former speeches have but hit your thoughts,

Which can interpret farther. Only I say

Things have been strangely borne. The gracious Duncan

Was pitied of Macbeth. Marry, he was dead!

And the right valiant Banquo walked too late;   5

Whom, you may say (if it please you) Fleance killed,

For Fleance fled. Men must not walk too late.

Who cannot want the thought how monstrous

It was for Malcolm and for Donalbain

To kill their gracious father? Damned fact!   10

How it did grieve Macbeth! Did he not straight,

In pious rage, the two delinquents tear,

That were the slaves of drink and thralls of sleep?

Was that not nobly done? Ay, and wisely too!

For 'twould have angered any heart alive   15

To hear the men deny't. So that I say

He has borne all things well; and I do think

That, had he Duncan's sons under his key

(As, an't please heaven, he shall not), they should find

What 'twere to kill a father. So should Fleance.   20

But peace! For from broad words, and 'cause he failed

His presence at the tyrant's feast, I hear

Macduff lives in disgrace. Sir, can you tell

Where he bestows himself?

LORD The son of Duncan,   25

From whom this tyrant holds the due of birth,

Lives in the English court, and is received

Scene 6   [*Forres. The palace*]

Enter LENNOX *and a* LORD

LENNOX   My recent words have but hinted your thoughts,

Which draw their own conclusions; only I say

Things have been strangely done. The gracious Duncan

Was pitied by Macbeth; but, no wonder, he was dead.

And the truly valiant Banquo went walking too late at night,   5

And was killed, so it seems, by his own son Fleance,

Who has since fled. Men must not walk too late.

Who cannot but think how monstrous

It was for Malcolm and for Donalbain

To kill their gracious father? Damned deed!   10

How it did grieve Macbeth! Did he not straightaway,

In pious rage, kill the suspected officers

That were in a drunken stupor and asleep?

Was that not nobly done? Yes, and wisely, too;

For 'twould have angered any heart alive   15

To hear the men deny it. So, I say

Macbeth has borne things well; and I think

That had he Duncan's sons under lock and key

(As, it please heaven, he shall not), they should find

What it was to kill a father; so should Fleance.   20

But listen, for unguarded speech and because he failed

To appear at the usurper's feast, I hear that

Macduff lives in disgrace. Sir, can you tell me

Where he has taken refuge?

LORD   The son of Duncan,   25

From whom this tyrant withholds his birthright,

Lives in the English court and is received

Of the most pious Edward with such grace

That the malevolence of fortune nothing

Takes from his high respect. Thither Macduff   30

Is gone to pray the holy King upon his aid

To wake Northumberland and warlike Siward;

That by the help of these (with Him above

To ratify the work) we may again

Give to our tables meat, sleep to our nights,   35

Free from our feasts and banquets bloody knives,

Do faithful homage and receive free honors—

All which we pine for now. And this report

Hath so exasperate the King that he

Prepares for some attempt of war.   40

LENNOX Sent he to Macduff?

LORD He did; and with an absolute "Sir, not I!"

The cloudy messenger turns me his back

And hums, as who should say, "You'll rue the time

That clogs me with this answer."   45

LENNOX And that well might

Advise him to a caution to hold what distance

His wisdom can provide. Some holy angel

Fly to the court of England and unfold

His message ere he come, that a swift blessing   50

May soon return to this our suffering country

Under a hand accursed!

LORD I'll send my prayers with him.

Exeunt

By the most pious King Edward with such favor

That his misfortunes in no way

Diminish the respect he is shown. And there Macduff   30

Has gone to seek King Edward's aid

To rouse the people of North and warlike Siward,

That with their help, and with God's approval

Of their work, we may again in Scotland

Give meat to our tables, sleep to our nights,   35

Free from our feasts' and banquets' bloody knives,

Do sincere homage and receive unbought honors—

All of which we long for now. This report of favor shown Malcolm

Has so enraged Macbeth that he

Prepares for some attempt at war.   40

LENNOX Has he sent for Macduff?

LORD He has; and with a firm "Sir, not I"

The sullen messenger returns

And mutters, as one who'd say, "I'm not hurrying back

With this unwelcome answer."   45

LENNOX And well might Macduff

Learn to be cautious, to keep as great a distance

As in his wisdom he can manage. Some holy angel

Fly to the court of England and disclose

This message so he'll come, that a swift blessing   50

May soon return to this our country suffering

Under a hateful hand.

LORD I'll send my prayers with him.

They exit

Act Four

Scene 1 [*A cavern. In the middle, a boiling cauldron*]

Thunder. Enter the three WITCHES

FIRST WITCH Thrice the brinded cat hath mewed.

SECOND WITCH Thrice and once the hedge-pig whined.

THIRD WITCH Harpier cries; 'tis time, 'tis time.

FIRST WITCH Round about the cauldron go;

    In the poisoned entrails throw.   5

    Toad, that under cold stone

    Days and nights has thirty-one

    Sweltered venom sleeping got,

    Boil thou first in the charmed pot.

ALL Double, double, toil and trouble;   10

    Fire burn, and cauldron bubble.

SECOND WITCH Fillet of fenny snake,

    In the cauldron boil and bake;

    Eye of newt, and toe of frog,

    Wool of bat, and tongue of dog,   15

    Adder's fork, and blindworm's sting,

    Lizard's leg, and howlet's wing;

    For a charm of powerful trouble

    Like a hell-broth boil and bubble.

ALL Double, double, toil and trouble;   20

    Fire burn, and cauldron bubble.

THIRD WITCH Scale of dragon, tooth of wolf

    Witch's mummy, maw and gulf

    Of the ravined salt-sea shark,

    Root of hemlock, digged in the dark;   25

    Liver of blaspheming Jew,

Act Four

Scene 1 [*A cavern. In the middle, a boiling cauldron*]

Thunder. Enter the three WITCHES

FIRST WITCH Three times the striped cat has mewed.

SECOND WITCH One more than that the hedgehog whined.

THIRD WITCH The Harpy cries, "It's time, it's time."

FIRST WITCH Round about the cauldron go;

    In the poisoned entrails throw.   5

    Toad, that under cold stone

    Has for days and nights thirty-one

    Sweated venom while sleeping not,

    You'll boil first in our charmed pot.

ALL Double, double, toil and trouble;   10

    Fire burn, and cauldron bubble.

SECOND WITCH A slice now of marshy snake,

    In the cauldron boil and bake;

    Eye of newt, and toe of frog,

    Wool of bat, and tongue of dog,   15

    Adder's fork, and slowworm's sting,

    Lizard's leg, and owlet's wing,

    For a charm of powerful trouble,

    Like a hell-broth boil and bubble.

ALL Double, double, toil and trouble;   20

    Fire burn, and cauldron bubble.

THIRD WITCH Scale of dragon, tooth of wolf,

    Powdered flesh, belly and mouth

    Of the gorged salt-sea shark,

    Root of hemlock dug in the dark,   25

    Liver of blaspheming Jew,

Gall of goat, and slips of yew

Slivered in the moon's eclipse;

Nose of Turk and Tartar's lips;

Finger of birth-strangled babe   30

Ditch-delivered by a drab;

Make the gruel thick and slab.

Add thereto a tiger's chaudron

For the ingredience of our cauldron.

ALL   Double, double, toil and trouble;   35

Fire burn, and cauldron bubble.

SECOND WITCH   Cool it with a baboon's blood

Then the charm is firm and good.

Enter HECATE *and the other three* WITCHES

HECATE   O, well done! I commend your pains,

And every one shall share in the gains.   40

And now about the cauldron sing

Like elves and fairies in a ring,

Enchanting all that you put in.

Music and a song, "Black Spirits," *etc.*

Exit HECATE

SECOND WITCH   By the pricking of my thumbs,

Something wicked this way comes.   45

Open locks,

Whoever knocks!

Enter MACBETH

MACBETH   How now, you secret, black, and midnight hags?

What is't you do?

ALL   A deed without a name.   50

Gall of goat, and bark of yew

Slivered in the moon's eclipse,

Nose of Turk, and Tartar's lips,

Finger of babe strangled at birth,   30

Born in a ditch by a slut of no worth,

Make thick the gruel and let settle;

Add thereto a tiger's bowels,

For the ingredients of our kettle.

ALL   Double, double, toil and trouble   35

Fire burn, and cauldron bubble.

SECOND WITCH   Cool it with a baboon's blood,

Then the charm is firm and good.

Enter HECATE *to the other three* WITCHES

HECATE   O, well done! I commend your pains,

And everyone shall share the gains.   40

And now about the cauldron sing,

Like elves and fairies in a ring,

Enchanting all that you put in.

Music and a song, "Black Spirits," *etc.*

Exit HECATE

SECOND WITCH   The prickling of my thumbs

Tells me something wicked this way comes.   45

Open locks,

Whoever knocks!

Enter MACBETH

MACBETH   How now, you secret, black and midnight hags!

What are you doing?

ALL   A deed without a name.   50

MACBETH   I conjure you by that which you profess
    (However you come to know it) answer me.
    Though you untie the winds and let them fight
    Against the churches; though the yeasty waves
    Confound and swallow navigation up;   55
    Though bladed corn be lodged and trees blown down;
    Though castles topple on their warders' heads;
    Though palaces and pyramids do slope
    Their heads to their foundations; though the treasure
    Of nature's germens tumble all together,   60
    Even till destruction sicken—answer me
    To what I ask you.
FIRST WITCH   Speak.
SECOND WITCH   Demand.
THIRD WITCH   We'll answer.   65
FIRST WITCH   Say, if thou hadst hear it from our mouths
    Or from our masters.
MACBETH   Call 'em! Let me see 'em.
FIRST WITCH   Pour in sow's blood, that hath eaten
    Her nine farrow; grease that's sweaten   70
    From the murderer's gibbet throw
    Into the flame.
ALL   Come, high or low;
    Thyself and office deftly show!
Thunder. FIRST APPARITION, *an armed head*
MACBETH   Tell me, thou unknown power—   75
FIRST WITCH   He knows thy thought.
    Hear his speech, but say thou naught.

MACBETH I summon you by those powers that you practice

(However you come by them) to answer me.

Though you untie the winds and let them fight

Against the churches; though the foamy waves

Destroy and swallow up the ships at sea;   55

Though unripe wheat be flattened, and trees blown down;

Though castles topple on their watchmen's heads,

Though palaces and pyramids do bend

Their heads to their foundations, though the treasury

Of nature's seeds tumble all together   60

Enough to satisfy chaos—answer me

What I ask of you.

FIRST WITCH Speak.

SECOND WITCH Demand.

THIRD WITCH We'll answer.   65

FIRST WITCH Say if you'd rather hear it from our mouths,

Or from our masters?

MACBETH Call them, let me see them.

FIRST WITCH Pour in blood from the sow that ate

Her own litter; grease that's sweated   70

From a murderer's gallows, throw

Into the flame.

ALL Come high and low;

Yourself and function clearly show.

Thunder. FIRST APPARITION, *a head wearing a helmet*

MACBETH Tell me, you unknown power—   75

FIRST WITCH He knows your thought.

Let him speak, and speak you not.

FIRST APPARITION Macbeth! Macbeth! Macbeth! Beware Macduff;
　　Beware the Thane of Fife. Dismiss me. Enough.

He descends

MACBETH Whate'er thou art, for thy good caution thanks!　　　80
　　Thou hast harped my fear aright. But one word more—
FIRST WITCH He will not be commanded. Here's another,
　　More potent than the first.

Thunder. SECOND APPARITION, *a bloody child*

SECOND APPARITION Macbeth! Macbeth! Macbeth!
MACBETH Had I three ears, I'd hear thee.　　　　　　　　85
SECOND APPARITION Be bloody, bold, and resolute; laugh to scorn
　　The power of man, for none of woman born
　　Shall harm Macbeth.

He descends

MACBETH Then live, Macduff. What need I fear of thee?
　　But yet I'll make assurance double sure　　　　　　　90
　　And take a bond of fate. Thou shalt not live!
　　That I may tell pale-hearted fear it lies
　　And sleep in spite of thunder.

Thunder. THIRD APPARITION, *a child crowned with a tree*
　　in his hand

　　What is this
　　That rises like the issue of a king　　　　　　　　　95
　　And wears upon his baby-brow the round
　　And top of sovereignty?
ALL Listen, but speak not to it.
THIRD APPARITION Be lion-mettled, proud, and take no care
　　Who chafes, who frets, or where conspirers are.　　　100
　　Macbeth shall never vanquished be until

114

FIRST APPARITION Macbeth! Macbeth! Macbeth! Beware Macduff!

    Beware the Thane of Fife. Dismiss me. Enough.

He descends

MACBETH Whatever you are, for your good warning, thanks!   80

    You have guessed my fear aright. But one word more—

FIRST WITCH He will not be commanded. But here's another,

    Still more potent than the first.

Thunder. SECOND APPARITION, *a bloody child*

SECOND APPARITION Macbeth! Macbeth! Macbeth!

MACBETH I don't need three ears to hear you.   85

SECOND APPARITION Be bloody, bold, and resolute; laugh to scorn

    The power of man, for none of woman born

    Shall harm Macbeth.

He descends

MACBETH Then live, Macduff; I don't need to fear you!

    But just to make assurance doubly sure,   90

    And make a contract with fate, you shall not live,

    So that I may show my fears are groundless,

    And sleep in spite of thunder.

Thunder. THIRD APPARITION, *a child crowned, with a tree*

    in his hand

    What is this,

    That rises like the offspring of a king,   95

    And wears upon his baby's brow

    The crown of sovereignty?

ALL Listen, but do not speak to it.

THIRD APPARITION Be lion-hearted, proud, and take no heed

    Of who is angry or complains or conspires.   100

    Macbeth shall never vanquished be until

Great Birnam Wood to high Dunsinane Hill
Shall come against him.

He descends

MACBETH That will never be.

    Who can impress the forest, bid the tree   105

    Unfix his earth-bound root? Sweet bodements, good!

    Rebellion's head rise never till the Wood

    Of Birnam rise, and our high-placed Macbeth

    Shall live the lease of nature, pay his breath

    To time and mortal custom. Yet my heart   110

    Throbs to know one thing. Tell me, if your art

    Can tell so much, shall Banquo's issue ever

    Reign in this kingdom?

ALL Seek to know no more.

MACBETH I will be satisfied. Deny me this,   115

    And an eternal curse fall on you! Let me know.

Cauldron sinks. Oboes play

    Why sinks that cauldron? And what noise is this?

FIRST WITCH Show!

SECOND WITCH Show!

THIRD WITCH Show!   120

ALL Show his eyes, and grieve his heart!

    Come like shadows, so depart!

       A show of eight KINGS, *the eighth with a glass in his hand,*
       and BANQUO *last*

MACBETH Thou are too like the spirit of Banquo. Down!

    Thy crown does sear mine eyeballs. And thy air,

    Thou other gold-bound brow, is like the first.   125

    A third is like the former. Filthy hags!

Great Birnam Wood to high Dunsinane Hill

Shall come against him.

He descends

MACBETH   That will never be:

Who can conscript the forest, bid the tree   105

Unfix his earth-bound root? Sweet prophecies, good!

Rebellion's head will never rise till the Wood

Of Birnam rise, and our high-placed Macbeth

Shall live out his natural life and breathe

Until the normal time to die. Yet my heart   110

Throbs to know one thing: tell me, if your art

Can tell so much, shall Banquo's offspring ever

Reign in this kingdom?

ALL   Seek to know no more.

MACBETH   I will know all. Deny me this,   115

And an eternal curse fall on you! Let me know.

Cauldron sinks. Oboes play

Why sinks that cauldron? What music is this?

FIRST WITCH   Show!

SECOND WITCH   Show!

THIRD WITCH   Show!   120

ALL   Show his eyes, and grieve his heart.

Come like shadows; so depart.

A procession of eight KINGS, *the last with a mirror in his hand,*

the GHOST *of* BANQUO *following*

MACBETH   You are too like the spirit of Banquo; down!

Your crown does sear my eyeballs. And your air,

The second gold-bound brow, is like the first.   125

A third is like the former. Filthy hags!

Why do you show me this? A fourth? Start, eyes!

What, will the line stretch out to the crack of doom?

Another yet? A seventh? I'll see no more.

And yet the eighth appears, who bears a glass 130

Which shows me many more; and some I see

That twofold balls and treble scepters carry.

Horrible sight! Now I see 'tis true;

For the blood-boltered Banquo smiles upon me

And points at them for his. What, is this so? 135

FIRST WITCH Ay, sir, all this is so. But why

Stands Macbeth thus amazedly?

Come, sisters, cheer we up his sprites

And show the best of our delights.

I'll charm the air to give a sound 140

While you perform your antic round,

That this great king may kindly say

Our duties did his welcome pay.

Music. The WITCHES *dance and vanish*

MACBETH Where are they? Gone? Let this pernicious hour

Stand aye accursed in the calendar! 145

Come in, without there!

Enter LENNOX

LENNOX What's your Grace's will?

MACBETH Saw you the Weird Sisters?

LENNOX No, my lord.

MACBETH Came they not by you? 150

LENNOX No indeed, my lord.

MACBETH Infected be the air whereon they ride,

And damned all those that trust them! I did hear

Why do you show me this? A fourth? Burst, eyes!

What, will the line stretch out to the crack of doom?

Another yet? A seventh? I'll see no more.

And yet the eighth appears who bears a glass   130

That shows me many more, and some I see

The twofold orbs and triple scepters carry.

Horrible sight! Now I see it's true,

For the blood-matted Banquo smiles upon me

And points to them as his. What, is this so?   135

FIRST WITCH Yes, sir, this is true. But why

Stand here so dumfoundedly?

Come, sisters, let us cheer him to see

All the best that we can be.

I'll charm the air to give a sound   140

While you perform your antic round,

That this great king may kindly say

Our duties did his welcome pay.

Music. The WITCHES *dance and vanish*

MACBETH Where are they? Gone? Let this ruinous hour

Stand forever accursed in the calendar!!   145

Come in, who's out there!

Enter LENNOX

LENNOX What is your Grace's will?

MACBETH Did you see the Weird Sisters?

LENNOX No, my lord.

MACBETH Didn't they pass by you?   150

LENNOX No, indeed, my lord.

MACBETH Let the air be infected on which they ride,

And damned all those that trust them. I did hear

The galloping of horse. Who was't came by?

LENNOX 'Tis two or three, my lord, that bring you word   155
    Macduff is fled to England.

MACBETH Fled to England?

LENNOX Ay, my good lord.

MACBETH [*Aside*] Time, thou anticipatest my dread exploits.

    The flighty purpose never is overtook   160

    Unless the deed go with it. From this moment

    The very feelings of my heart shall be

    The firstlings of my hand. And even now,

    To crown my thoughts with acts, be it thought and done!

    The castle of Macduff I will surprise,   165

    Seize upon Fife, give to the edge of the sword

    His wife, his babes, and all unfortunate souls

    That trace him in his line. No boasting like a fool!

    This deed I'll do before this purpose cool.

    But no more sights! [*Aloud*] Where are these gentlemen?   170

    Come, bring me where they are.

                                  Exeunt

Scene 2 [*Fife. Macduff's castle*]

                  Enter LADY MACDUFF, *her* SON, *and* ROSS

LADY MACDUFF What had he done to make him fly the land?

ROSS You must have patience, madam.

LADY MACDUFF He had none.

    His flight was madness. When our actions do not,

    Our fears do make us traitors.   5

ROSS You know not

    Whether it was his wisdom or his fear.

The galloping of horses. Who was it came by?

LENNOX It's two or three, my lord, that bring you word: 155

Macduff has fled to England.

MACBETH Fled to England?

LENNOX Yes, my good lord.

MACBETH [*Aside*] Time, you intercept my dreadful deeds.

Unless we act on our purpose the moment we think of it,

The chance is lost. From this moment,

The first impulse of my heart shall be

The first impulse of my hand. And even now,

To crown my thoughts with acts, be it thought and be it done!

The castle of Macduff I will surprise,   165

Seize from Fife, give to the edge of the sword

His wife, his babes, and all unfortunate souls

That trace him in their line. No boasting like a fool;

This deed I'll do before its purpose cools.

No more witches' shows! [*Aloud*] Where are these gentlemen?   170

Come, bring me where they are.

                              They exit

Scene 2 [*Fife. Macduff's castle*]

                    Enter LADY MACDUFF, *her* SON, *and* ROSS

LADY MACDUFF What had he done to make him fly the land?

ROSS You must have self-control, madam.

LADY MACDUFF He had none.

His flight was madness. Even when our acts are free of guilt,

Our fears make us seem traitors.   5

ROSS You know not

Whether it was his wisdom or his fear.

LADY MACDUFF Wisdom? To leave his wife, to leave his babes,

His mansion, and his titles, in a place

From whence himself does fly? He loves us not,   10

He wants the natural touch. For the poor wren,

The most diminutive of birds, will fight,

Her young ones in her nest, against the owl.

All is the fear and nothing is the love,

As little is the wisdom, where the flight   15

So runs against all reason.

ROSS My dearest coz,

I pray you school yourself. But, for your husband,

He is noble, wise, judicious, and best knows

The fits of the season. I dare not speak much further: 20

But cruel are the times, when we are traitors

And do not know ourselves; when we hold rumor

From what we fear, yet know not what we fear,

But float upon a wild and violent sea

Each way and none. I take my leave of you.   25

Shall not be long but I'll be here again.

Things at the worst will cease, or else climb upward

To what they were before. My pretty cousin,

Blessing upon you!

LADY MACDUFF Fathered he is, and yet he's fatherless.   30

ROSS I am so much a fool, should I stay longer,

It would be my disgrace and your discomfort.

I take my leave at once.

Exit

LADY MACDUFF Sirrah, your father's dead;

And what will you do now? How will you live?   35

LADY MACDUFF Wisdom? To leave his wife, to leave his babes,

    His mansion and possessions in a place

    From which he himself flies? He loves us not;   10

    He lacks the natural touch. Even the poor wren,

    The most diminutive of birds, will fight,

    When her young are in the nest, against the owl.

    All is fear, and nothing is love,

    Still less wisdom, when his flight   15

    So runs against all wisdom.

ROSS Dearest cousin,

    I pray you, control yourself. As for your husband,

    He is noble, wise, judicious, and knows best

    The climate of these times. I dare not speak much further;   20

    But cruel are the times, when we are called traitors

    And do not know it ourselves; when we believe rumors

    Out of fear, yet know not what we fear,

    But float upon a wild and violent sea,

    Tossed this way and that. I must say goodbye now.   25

    But before long, I'll be back.

    Things, at the worst, will cease, or else get better,

    The way they were before. My pretty cousin,

    Blessing upon you!

LADY MACDUFF My son has a father, and yet he's fatherless.   30

ROSS If I stay longer, I'll make a fool of myself,

    I would weep, and you would be embarrassed.

    So I must go at once.

                                  Exit ROSS

LADY MACDUFF My son, your father's dead,

    And what will you do now? How will you live?   35

SON As birds do, mother.

LADY MACDUFF What, with worms and flies?

SON With what I get, I mean; and so do they.

LADY MACDUFF Poor bird! Thou'dst never fear the net nor lime,

    The pitfall nor the gin. 40

SON Why should I, mother?

    Poor birds they are not set for.

    My father is not dead, for all your saying.

LADY MACDUFF Yes, he is dead. How wilt thou do for a father?

SON Nay, how will you do for a husband? 45

LADY MACDUFF Why, I can buy me twenty at any market.

SON Then you'll buy them to sell again.

LADY MACDUFF Thou speakest with all they wit; and yet, in faith,

    With wit enough for thee.

SON Was my father a traitor, mother? 50

LADY MACDUFF Ay, that he was!

SON What is a traitor?

LADY MACDUFF Why, one that swears and lies.

SON And be all traitors that do so?

LADY MACDUFF Every one that does so is a traitor and must 55

    be hanged.

SON And must they all be hanged that swear and lie?

LADY MACDUFF Every one.

SON Who must hang them?

LADY MACDUFF Why, the honest men. 60

SON Then the liars and swearers are fools; for there are liars and swearers

    enow to beat the honest men and hang up them.

LADY MACDUFF Now God help thee, poor monkey! But how wilt

    do for a father?

SON As birds do, mother.

LADY MACDUFF What, with worms and flies?

SON With what I find, I mean; and so do they.

LADY MACDUFF Poor bird, you would never fear the net or lime,

The snare or the trap.   40

SON Why should I, mother?

No one sets traps for poor birds.

My father is not dead, despite what you say.

LADY MACDUFF Yes, he is dead. What will you do for a father?

SON No, what will you do for a husband?   45

LADY MACDUFF Why, I can buy me twenty at any market.

SON Then, you'll buy them only to sell them.

LADY MACDUFF You speak with all your wit, and yet in truth,

With wit enough for your age.

SON Was my father a traitor, mother?   50

LADY MACDUFF Yes, that he was.

SON What is a traitor?

LADY MACDUFF Why, one that takes an oath and lies.

SON And are all who do that traitors?

LADY MACDUFF Every one that does so is a traitor, and must   55

be hanged.

SON And must they all be hanged that swear and lie?

LADY MACDUFF Every one.

SON Who must hang them?

LADY MACDUFF Why, the honest men.   60

SON Then the liars and swearers must be fools, for there are enough

of them to beat the honest men and hang them up.

LADY MACDUFF Now God help you, poor monkey! But what will you

do for a father?

SON If he were dead, you'ld weep for him. If you would not, it   65
    were a good sign that I should quickly have a new father.

LADY MACDUFF Poor prattler, how thou talkest!

Enter a MESSENGER

MESSENGER Bless you, fair dame! I am not to you known
    Though in your state of honor I am perfect.
    I doubt some danger does approach you nearly.   70
    If you will take a homely man's advice,
    Be not found here; hence, with your little ones.
    To fright you thus, methinks I am too savage;
    To do worse to you were fell cruelty,
    Which is too nigh your person. Heaven preserve you!   75
    I dare abide no longer.

Exit

LADY MACDUFF Whither should I fly?
    I have done no harm. But I remember now
    I am in this earthly world, where to do harm
    Is often laudable, to do good sometime   80
    Accounted dangerous folly. Why then, alas,
    Do I put up that womanly defense
    To say I have done no harm?

Enter MURDERERS

    What are these faces?

FIRST MURDERER Where is your husband?   85

LADY MACDUFF I hope, in no place so unsanctified
    Where such as thou mayest find him.

FIRST MURDERER He's a traitor.

SON Thou liest, thou shag-eared villain!

SON If he were dead, you'd weep for him. Still, if you would not weep, 65
    it were a good sign that I should quickly have a new father.

LADY MACDUFF Poor prattler, how you do talk!

Enter a MESSENGER

MESSENGER Bless you, fair lady! You do not know me,
    Though I know who you are.
    I fear that some harm does approach you soon. 70
    If you will take a simple man's advice,
    Don't be found here. Leave with your little ones.
    To scare you so, I feel I am too cruel,
    But not to warn you would be fiercely cruel,
    For danger now is close. Heaven help you! 75
    I dare stay no longer.

He exits

LADY MACDUFF Where should I go?
    I have done no harm. But then I remember
    This is how the world works, to do harm
    Is often applauded, to do good sometimes 80
    Seen as dangerous folly. Why then, alas,
    Should I erect that womanly defense
    And say I have done no harm?

Enter MURDERERS

    Who are you people?

FIRST MURDERER Where is your husband? 85

LADY MACDUFF I hope in no place so unholy
    That people like you could find him.

FIRST MURDERER He's a traitor.

SON You lie, you shag-haired villain!

127

FIRST MURDERER What, you egg! [*Stabs him*]   90
    Young fry of treachery!
SON He has killed me, mother.
    Run away, I pray you! [*Dies*]

> *Exit* LADY MACDUFF, *crying "Murder!" and*
> *perused by the* MURDERERS, *carrying off the boy's body*

Scene 3 [*England. In front of the King's palace*]

> *Enter* MALCOLM *and* MACDUFF

MALCOLM Let us seek out some desolate shade, and there
    Weep our sad bosoms empty.
MACDUFF Let us rather
    Hold fast the mortal sword and, like good men,
    Bestride our downfallen birthdom. Each new morn   5
    New widows howl, new orphans cry, new sorrows
    Strike heaven on the face, that it resounds
    As if it felt with Scotland and yelled out
    Like syllable of dolor.
MALCOLM What I believe, I'll wail;   10
    What know, believe; and what I can redress,
    As I shall find the time to friend, I will.
    What you have spoke, it may be so perchance.
    This tyrant, whose sole name blisters our tongues,
    Was once thought honest; you have loved him well;   15
    He hath not touched you yet. I am young; but
    Something you may deserve of him
            through me, and wisdom
    To offer up a weak, poor, innocent lamb

FIRST MURDERER What, you egg? [*Stabs him*]   90

    Young spawn of treachery!

SON He has killed me, mother.

    Escape, I beg you. [*Dies*]

                Exit LADY MACDUFF, *crying "Murder!" and*

          pursued by the MURDERERS, *carrying off the boy's body*

Scene 3 [*England. In front of the King's palace*]

              Enter MALCOLM *and* MACDUFF

MALCOLM Let us seek out some desolate shade and there

    Weep our sad hearts empty.

MACDUFF Let us rather

    Hold fast the deadly sword, like brave soldiers,

    Protecting our fallen country. Each new morn   5

    New widows howl, new orphans cry, new sorrows

    Strike heaven in the face, so that it resounds

    In sympathy with Scotland and yells out

    The same cries of grief.

MALCOLM What I believe, I'll grieve over;   10

    What I know, I'll believe; and what I set right,

    When I find the time right, I will.

    What you have said, it may perhaps be true.

    This tyrant, whose mere name blisters our tongues,

    Was once thought honest; you have loved him well;   15

    He has not harmed you yet. I am young, but you

    May hope to gain something from him through me, and

        it would be politic

    To offer up a weak, poor, innocent lamb

To appease an angry god.   20

MACDUFF I am not treacherous.

MALCOLM But Macbeth is.

    A good and virtuous nature may recoil

    In imperial charge. But I shall crave your pardon.

    That which you are, my thoughts cannot transpose.   25

    Angels are bright still, though the brightest fell.

    Though all things foul would weak the brows of grace,

    Yet grace must still look so.

MACDUFF I have lost my hopes.

MALCOLM Perchance even there where I did find my doubts.   30

    Why in that rawness left you wife and child,

    Those precious motives, those strong knots of love,

    Without leave-taking? I pray you,

    Let not my jealousies be your dishonors,

    But mine own safeties. You may be rightly just,   35

    Whatever I shall think.

MACDUFF Bleed, bleed, poor country!

    Great tyranny, lay thou thy basis sure,

    For goodness dare not check thee! Wear thou thy wrongs;

    The title is affeered! Fare thee well, lord.   40

    I would not be the villain that thou thinkest

    For the whole space that's in the tyrant's grasp

    And the rich East to boot.

MALCOLM Be not offended.

    I speak not as in absolute fear of you,   45

    I think our country sinks beneath the yoke,

    It weeps, it bleeds, and each new day a gash

    Is added to her wounds. I think withal

To appease an angry god.   20

MACDUFF   I am not treacherous.

MALCOLM   But Macbeth is.

A good and virtuous nature may recoil

At a royal command. But I should ask your pardon.

Whatever you are, my thoughts cannot change you.   25

Angels are bright still, though Lucifer did fall.

Though all things foul strive for the appearance of virtue,

Yet virtue still looks as it always has.

MACDUFF   I have lost all hope.

MALCOLM   Perhaps even in your flight did I find reason to doubt.   30

Why did you leave wife and child unprotected,

Those precious reasons, those strong knots of love,

Without even a goodbye? I pray you won't

Let my suspicions cast doubt on your honor;

See them as regard for my own safety. You may be truly just,   35

Whatever I may think.

MACDUFF   Bleed, bleed, poor country!

Great tyranny, lay your base in safety,

For goodness dare not check you! Wear your wrongs;

Their title is confirmed! Farewell, my lord.   40

I would not be the villain that you think

For the whole realm that's in the tyrant's grasp,

And the rich East to boot.

MALCOLM   Be not offended;

I speak not in complete mistrust of you.   45

I think our country sinks beneath the yoke.

It weeps, it bleeds, and each new day a gash

Is added to her wounds. I think, moreover,

There would be hands uplifted in my right:
And here from gracious England have I offer   50
Of goodly thousands. But, for all this,
When I shall tread upon the tyrant's head
Or wear it on my sword, yet my poor country
Shall have more vices than it had before,
More suffer and more sundry ways than ever,   55
By him that shall succeed.
MACDUFF What should he be?
MALCOLM It is myself I mean; in whom I know
All the particulars of vice so grafted
That, when they shall be opened, black Macbeth   60
Will seem as pure as snow, and the poor state
Esteem him as a lamb, being compared
With my confineless harms.
MACDUFF Not in the legions
Of horrid hell can come a devil more damned   65
In evils to top Macbeth.
MALCOLM I grant him bloody,
Luxurious, avaricious, false, deceitful,
Sudden, malicious, smacking of every sin
That has a name. But there's no bottom, none,   70
In my voluptuousness. Your wives, your daughters,
Your matrons, and your maids could not fill up
The cistern of my lust; and my desire
All continent impediments would overbear
That did oppose my will. Better Macbeth   75
Than such an one to reign.

There would be hands raised to back my claim;

And here from the gracious king have I an offer   50

Of thousands of men. But even so,

If ever I should tread upon the tyrant's head,

Or carry it on my sword, then my poor country

Will suffer more vices than it did before,

And in more ways than ever,   55

From the king who comes next.

MACDUFF Who should that be?

MALCOLM It is myself I mean; in whom I know

All the individual vices are so implanted

That, when they flower, the black Macbeth   60

Shall seem as pure as snow, and our poor land

Will view him as a lamb compared

With my boundless evils.

MACDUFF Nowhere in the legions

Of horrid hell can there be a devil more damned   65

In evils to top Macbeth.

MALCOLM I grant he's bloody,

Lustful, greedy, false, deceitful,

Impetuous, malicious, smacking of every sin

That has a name, but there's no bottom, none,   70

To my lechery: Your wives, your daughters,

Your matrons, and your maids could never fill up

The stagnant well of my lust; and my desire,

So incontinent, would overbear those

That did oppose my will. Better Macbeth   75

Than such a one should reign.

MACDUFF   Boundless intemperance

In nature is a tyranny. It hath been

The untimely emptying of the happy throne

And fall of many kings. But fear not yet   80

To take upon you what is yours. You may

Convey your pleasures in a spacious plenty,

And yet seem cold—the time you may so hoodwink.

We have willing dames enough. There cannot be

That vulture in you to devour so many   85

As will to greatness dedicate themselves,

Finding it so inclined.

MALCOLM   With this there grows

In my most ill-composed affection such

A staunchless avarice that, were I King,   90

I should cut off the nobles for their lands,

Desire his jewels, and this other's house,

And my more-having would be as a sauce

To make me hunger more, that I should forge

Quarrels unjust against the good and loyal,   95

Destroying them for wealth.

MACDUFF   This avarice

Sticks deeper, grows with more pernicious root

Than summer-seeming lust; and it hath been

The sword of our slain kings. Yet do not fear.   100

Scotland hath foisons to fill up your will

Of your mere own. All these are portable,

With other graces weighed.

MALCOLM   But I have none. The king-becoming graces,

As justice, verity, temperance, stableness,   105

MACDUFF Boundless intemperance

     Is tyranny in a man's nature. It has

     Caused the early end of many prosperous reigns,

     And fall of many kings. But do not fear   80

     To take what is yours. You may

     Secretly enjoy your pleasures in ample plenty

     And yet appear chaste—you may hoodwink the people.

     We have enough willing women. There cannot be

     A vulture in you that could devour as many   85

     As will offer themselves to the king,

     Finding him so inclined.

MALCOLM But with this lust there grows

     In my unbalanced character such

     An insatiable greed that, were I King,   90

     I should kill off the nobles for their lands,

     Desire this man's jewels, and this other's house;

     And, it would be just an appetizer

     To make me hunger more, so that I would shape

     Unjust quarrels against the good and the loyal,   95

     Destroying them for their wealth.

MACDUFF This greed

     Goes deeper, and grows with more dangerous root

     Than a summer's lust; and it has been

     The cause of our slain kings. Yet do not fear;   100

     Scotland has riches enough to fill up your desires,

     Merely from your own estates. All these sins are bearable,

     When weighed against your virtues.

MALCOLM But I have none. The kingly virtues,

     Such as justice, truth, self-control, constancy,   105

Bounty, perseverance, mercy, lowliness,

Devotion, patience, courage, fortitude,

I have no relish of them, but abound

In the division of each several crime,

Acting it many ways. Nay, had I power, I should   110

Pour the sweet milk of concord into hell,

Uproar the universal peace, confound

All unity on earth.

MACDUFF O Scotland, Scotland!

MALCOLM If such a one be fit to govern, speak.   115

I am as I have spoken.

MACDUFF Fit to govern?

No, not to live. O nation miserable,

With an untitled tyrant bloody-sceptered,

When shalt thou see thy wholesome days again,   120

Since that the truest issue of thy throne

By his own interdiction stands accursed

And does blaspheme his breed? Thy royal father

Was a most sainted king; the queen that bore thee,

Oftener upon her knees than on her feet,   125

Died every day she lived. Fare thee well!

These evils thou repeatest upon thyself

Have banished me from Scotland. O my breast,

Thy hope ends here!

MALCOLM Macduff, this noble passion,   130

Child of integrity, hath from my soul

Wiped the black scruples, reconciled my thoughts

To thy good truth and honor. Devilish Macbeth

By many of these trains hath sought to win me

Generosity, perseverance, mercy, humility,

Piety, patience, courage, fortitude—

I have no taste for them, but instead

Delight in variations of each crime,

Acting them out in many ways. If I had the power, I should   110

Pour the sweet milk of concord into hell,

Cause uproar in universal peace, destroy

All unity on earth.

MACDUFF O Scotland, Scotland!

MALCOLM If such a one is fit to govern, speak.   115

    I am what I said.

MACDUFF Fit to govern?

    No, not even to live! O miserable nation

    Ruled by a self-crowned, bloody-sceptered tyrant,

    When shall you see wholesome days again,   120

    Now that the true heir to the throne

    By his own censure stands accused,

    And does defame his family line? Your royal father

    Was a most sainted king; the queen that bore you,

    Oftener on her knees than on her feet,   125

    Prepared each day for the next life. Farewell.

    These evils you recite against yourself

    Have banished me from Scotland. O my heart,

    Your hope ends here.

MALCOLM Macduff, this noble display,   130

    Child of integrity, has from my soul

    Wiped away the black doubts and reconciled me

    To your good truth and honor. Devilish Macbeth

    By many of these plots has sought to entice me

Into his power; and modest wisdom plucks me   135
From over-credulous haste; but God above
Deal between thee and me! for even now
I put myself to thy direction and
Unspeak mine own detraction, here abjure
The taints and blames I laid upon myself   140
For strangers to my nature. I am yet
Unknown to woman, never was foresworn,
Scarcely have coveted what was mine own,
At no time broke my faith, would not betray
The devil to his fellow, and delight   145
No less in truth than life. My first false speaking
Was this upon myself. What I am truly,
Is thine and my poor country's to command.
Whither indeed, before thy here-approach,
Old Siward with ten thousand warlike men   150
Already at a point was setting forth.
Now we'll together; and the chance of goodness
Be like our warranted quarrel! Why are you silent?
MACDUFF Such welcome and unwelcome things at once
    'Tis hard to reconcile.   155

Enter a DOCTOR

MALCOLM Well, more anon.
    Comes the king forth, I pray you?
DOCTOR Ay, sir. There are a crew of wretched souls
    That stay his cure. Their malady convinces
    The great assay of art; but at his touch,   160
    Such sanctity hath heaven given his hand,
    They presently amend.

Into his power, and prudent caution pulls me back 135
From overgulible haste; but only God above
Will direct our dealings! As of now,
I put myself under your direction and
Withdraw the slanders I spoke; here renounce
The stains and blames I laid upon myself, 140
As foreign to my nature. In fact, I am still
A virgin, nor have I ever lied;
I scarcely covet even what is mine,
I've never been disloyal, would not betray
Even the devil to his fellows, and delight 145
No less in truth than in life—my first falsehoods
Were these I spoke against myself. What I truly am
Is yours and my poor country's to command;
Where, indeed, before you came here,
Old Siward, with ten thousand warlike men 150
Fully armed, was setting forth.
Now we'll go together, and our chance of success
May match the justice of our cause. Why are you silent?

MACDUFF Such welcome and unwelcome news at once.
    It's hard to reconcile. 155

Enter a DOCTOR

MALCOLM Well, more later.
    Is the King on his way here?

DOCTOR Yes, sir; there are a crew of wretched souls
    That wait for him to cure them. Their sickness defeats
    The best efforts of medical skill; but at the King's touch, 160
    Heaven has so sanctified his hand,
    They are immediately cured.

MALCOLM I thank you, doctor.

Exit DOCTOR

MACDUFF What's the disease he means?

MALCOLM 'Tis called the evil: 165

    A most miraculous work in this good king,

    Which often since my here-remain in England

    I have seen him do. How he solicits heaven

    Himself best knows; but strangely-visited people,

    All swollen and ulcerous, pitiful to the eye,   170

    The mere despair of surgery, he cures,

    Hanging a golden stamp about their necks,

    Put on with holy prayers; and 'tis spoken,

    To the succeeding royalty he leaves

    The healing benediction. With this strange virtue,   175

    He hath a heavenly gift of prophecy,

    And sundry blessings hang about his throne

    That speak him full of grace.

Enter ROSS

MACDUFF See who comes here.

MALCOLM My countryman; but yet I know him not.   180

MACDUFF My ever gentle cousin, welcome hither.

MALCOLM I know him now. Good God, betimes remove

    The means that makes us strangers!

ROSS Sir, amen.

MACDUFF Stands Scotland where it did?   185

ROSS Alas, poor country,

    Almost afraid to know itself! It cannot

    Be called our mother, but our grave; where nothing,

    But who knows nothing, is once seen to smile;

MALCOLM I thank you, doctor.

Exit DOCTOR

MACDUFF What is the disease he means?

MALCOLM It's called the Evil;   165

    The cure is a miraculous work by this good king,

    Which often, since my stay here in England,

    I've seen him do. How he appeals to heaven

    Only he himself knows; but horribly afflicted people,

    All swollen and ulcerous, pitiful to the eye,   170

    The utter despair of surgeons, he cures,

    Hanging a golden coin about their necks,

    Saying holy prayers; and it's said

    He leaves to succeeding royalty

    The blessing of healing. To this strange power,   175

    He adds a heavenly gift of prophecy,

    And other blessings hang about his throne

    That show him to be full of grace.

Enter ROSS

MACDUFF Look who's coming now.

MALCOLM My countryman, but yet I do not know him.   180

MACDUFF My noble cousin, welcome here.

MALCOLM I know him now. Good God, quickly remove

    That tyrant who has made us strangers.

ROSS Sir, amen!

MACDUFF How stand things in Scotland now?   185

ROSS Ah, poor country,

    Almost afraid to know itself. You cannot

    Call it our mother now, but our grave, where no one

    But those who know nothing could smile;

Where sighs and groans, and shrieks that rent the air, 190

Are made, not marked; where violent sorrow seems

A modern ecstasy. The dead man's knell

Is there scarce asked for who; and good men's lives

Expire before the flowers in their caps,

Dying or ere they sicken. 195

MACDUFF O, relation

Too nice, and yet too true!

MALCOLM What's the newest grief?

ROSS That of an hour's age doth hiss the speaker;

Each minute teems a new one. 200

MACDUFF How does my wife?

ROSS Why, well.

MACDUFF And all my children?

ROSS Well too.

MACDUFF The tyrant has not battered at their peace? 205

ROSS No; they were well at peace when I did leave 'em.

MACDUFF Be not a niggard of your speech. How goes it?

ROSS When I came hither to transport the tidings

Which I have heavily borne, there ran a rumor

Of many worthy fellows that were out; 210

Which was to my belief witnessed the rather

For that I saw the tyrant's power afoot.

Now is the time for help. Your eye in Scotland

Would create soldiers, make our women fight

To doff their dire distresses. 215

MALCOLM Be it their comfort,

We are coming thither. Gracious England hath

Lent us good Siward and ten thousand men.

Where sighs and groans and shrieks that tear the air   190
Pass unnoticed; where violent sorrow has become
A common emotion. The tolling of funeral bells
Prompts no one to ask for whom, and good men's lives
Expire before the flowers in their caps,
Killed off before they wither.   195
MACDUFF   O report
    Too precise, and yet too true!
MALCOLM   What's the newest wrong?
ROSS   That any tale over an hour old brings hisses,
    Because each minute gives birth to a new one.   200
MACDUFF   How is my wife?
ROSS   She's well.
MACDUFF   And all my children?
ROSS   Well, too.
MACDUFF   The tyrant has not battered at their peace?   205
ROSS   No, they were at peace when I left them.
MACDUFF   Don't be stingy with your report; tell us more.
ROSS   When I came here with my report,
    Which I have sadly carried, there ran a rumor
    That many worthy men had taken up arms against Macbeth,   210
    My belief in which was confirmed
    Because I saw the tyrant's forces on the march.
    Now is the time to help. Your appearance in Scotland
    Would create new soldiers and make our women fight
    To end their dreadful fears.   215
MALCOLM   If it will make them feel better,
    We are on our way there. The gracious English king has
    Lent us the good Siward and ten thousand men.

An older and a better soldier none
That Christendom gives out.   220
ROSS   Would I could answer
This comfort with the like! But I have words
That would be howled out in the desert air,
Where hearing should not latch them.
MACDUFF   What concern they?   225
The general cause? Or is it a fee-grief
Due to some single breast?
ROSS   No mind that's honest
But in it shares some woe, though the main part
Pertains to you alone.   230
MACDUFF   If it be mine,
Keep it not from me, quickly let me have it.
ROSS   Let not your ears despise my tongue forever,
Which shall possess them with the heaviest sound
That ever yet they heard.   235
MACDUFF   Humh! I guess at it.
ROSS   Your castle is surprised; your wife and babes
Savagely slaughtered. To relate the manner,
Were, on the quarry of these murdered deer,
To add the death of you.   240
MALCOLM   Merciful heaven!
What, man! Ne'er pull your hat upon your brows.
Give sorrow words. The grief that does not speak
Whispers the o'erfraught heart and bids it break.
MACDUFF   My children too?   245
ROSS   Wife, children, servants, all
That could be found.

A more experienced and better soldier is not known

Throughout Christendom.   220

ROSS I wish I could match

This good news with more. But I have words

That should be howled out in the desert air,

Where hearing could not catch them.

MACDUFF What do they concern?   225

Is it public affairs or some private matter

That concerns a single person?

ROSS Any honorable person

Would share in this woe, but mainly

It pertains to you alone.   230

MACDUFF If it is mine,

Then do not keep it from me; quickly let me have it.

ROSS Let not your ears despise my tongue forever,

Which shall possess them with the saddest words

That ever yet they heard.   235

MACDUFF Humh! I think I know.

ROSS Your castle was suddenly attacked, your wife and children

Savagely slaughtered. To report how

Would be, to the heap of these murdered deer,

To add your death.   240

MALCOLM Merciful heaven!

What, Macduff, don't hide your face:

Give words to your sorrow. The grief that does not speak

Whispers to the overburdened heart and bids it break.

MACDUFF My children, too?   245

ROSS Wife, children, servants, all

That could be found.

MACDUFF   And I must be from thence?

  My wife killed too?

ROSS   I have said.   250

MALCOLM   Be comforted.

  Let's make us medicines of our great revenge

  To cure this deadly grief.

MACDUFF   He has no children. All my pretty ones?

  Did you say all? O hell-kite! All?   255

  What, all my pretty chickens and their dam

  At one fell swoop?

MALCOLM   Dispute it like a man.

MACDUFF   I shall do so;

  But I must also feel it as a man.   260

  I cannot but remember such things were

  That were most precious to me. Did heaven look on

  And would not take their part? Sinful Macduff,

  They were all struck for thee! Naught that I am,

  Not for their own demerits, but for mine,   265

  Fell slaughter on their souls. Heaven rest them now!

MALCOLM   Be this the whetstone of your sword. Let grief

  Convert to anger; blunt not the heart, enrage it.

MACDUFF   O, I could play the woman with mine eyes

  And braggart with my tongue! But, gentle heavens,   270

  Cut short all intermission. Front to front

  Bring thou this fiend of Scotland and myself.

  Within my sword's length set him. If he scape,

  Heaven forgive him too!

MACDUFF And I had to be away!

    My wife killed, too?

ROSS As I said.   250

MALCOLM Be comforted with this:

    We'll make medicines of our great revenge

    To cure this deadly grief.

MACDUFF He has no children. All my pretty ones?

    Did you say all? O hellish hawk! All?   255

    What, all my pretty chickens and their mother,

    At one fell swoop?

MALCOLM Withstand your grief, like a man.

MACDUFF I shall do so,

    But I must also feel it as a man.   260

    I cannot help remember such things

    That were the most precious to me. Did heaven look on

    And not take their side? Sinful Macduff,

    They were killed because of you. Worthless as I am,

    Not for their faults, but for mine,   265

    Slaughter fell upon their souls. Heaven rest them now.

MALCOLM Let this grief be the whetstone of your sword. Let grief

    Convert to anger; blunt not the heart, but enrage it.

MACDUFF O, I could weep with my eyes and play

    The braggart with my tongue. But, gentle heavens,   270

    Cut short all delay. Bring me face to face

    With this fiend of Scotland, just myself

    Within my sword's length set him. If he escape,

    Heaven forgive him too!

MALCOLM This tune goes manly. 275

    Come, go we to the King. Our power is ready;

    Our lack is nothing but our leave. Macbeth

    Is ripe for shaking, and the powers above

    Put on their instruments. Receive what cheer you may

    The night is long that never finds a day. 280

Exeunt

MALCOLM   This is a manly tune.   275

    Come, we go to the King. Our army is ready;

    We need only take our leave. Macbeth

    Is ready to be shaken off the tree, and the powers above

    Arm themselves. Receive what comfort you may;

    No night is so long that never finds the day.   280

They exit

Act Five

Scene 1 [*Macbeth's palace, Dunsiane*]

Enter a DOCTOR *and a* GENTLEWOMAN

DOCTOR I have two nights watched with you, but can
perceive no truth in your report. When was it she
last walked?

GENTLEWOMAN Since his Majesty went into the field I have seen her
rise from her bed, throw her nightgown upon her, unlock her closet, 5
take forth paper, fold it, write upon it, read it, afterwards seal it, and
again return to bed; yet all this while in a most fast sleep.

DOCTOR A great perturbation in nature, to receive at once the benefit of
sleep and do the effects of watching! In this slumbery agitation,
besides her walking and other actual performances, what, at any 10
time, have you heard her say?

GENTLEWOMAN That, sir, which I will not report after her.

DOCTOR You may to me, and 'tis most meet you should.

GENTLEWOMAN Neither to you nor any one, having no witness to
confirm my speech. 15

Enter LADY MACBETH *with a taper*

Lo you, here she comes! This is her very guise; and, upon
my life, fast asleep! Observe her; stand close.

DOCTOR How came she by that light?

GENTLEWOMAN Why, it stood by her. She has light by her continually.
'Tis her command. 20

DOCTOR You see her eyes are open.

GENTLEWOMAN Ay, but their sense are shut.

DOCTOR What is it she does now? Look how she rubs her hands.

150

Act Five

Scene 1 [*Macbeth's palace, Dunsiane*]

Enter a DOCTOR *and a* GENTLEWOMAN

DOCTOR I have stayed awake for two nights with you, but have seen no evidence of what you report. When was it she last walked in her sleep?

GENTLEWOMAN Ever since his Majesty went into battle, I have seen her rise from her bed, put on her dressing gown, unlock her desk, take 5 out some paper, fold it, write on it, read it, then seal it, and again return to bed; and all the while in a deep sleep.

DOCTOR A great disturbance in her nature, to sleep and at the same time act as though she were awake. In this sleeping activity, besides her walking and other deeds, what, at any time, have you heard 10 her say?

GENTLEWOMAN That, sir, which I will not repeat in her words.

DOCTOR You may tell me, and it is proper that you should.

GENTLEWOMAN Not to you or anyone else, having no witness to confirm what I say. 15

Enter LADY MACBETH *with a candle*

Look, here she comes. This is how she usually behaves; and, upon my life, fast asleep. Observe her, but stay hidden.

DOCTOR Where did she get that candle?

GENTLEWOMAN Why, it was near her bed. She always keeps one there. It is her command. 20

DOCTOR You can see that her eyes are open.

GENTLEWOMAN Yes, but she doesn't see anything.

DOCTOR What is she doing now? Look how she rubs her hands.

GENTLEWOMAN It is an accustomed action with her, to seem thus washing
    her hands. I have known her continue in this a quarter of an hour. 25
LADY MACBETH Yet here's a spot.
DOCTOR Hark, she speaks! I will set down what comes from her, to
    satisfy my remembrance the more strongly.
LADY MACBETH Out, damned spot! Out, I say! One; two. Why then
    'tis time to do it. Hell is murky. Fie, my lord, fie! A soldier, and 30
    afeard? What need we fear who knows it, when none can call our
    power to accompt? Yet who would have thought the old man to
    have so much blood in him?
DOCTOR Do you mark that?
LADY MACBETH The Thane of Fife had a wife. Where is she now? 35
    What, will these hands ne'er be clean? No more o' that, my lord,
    no more o' that! You mar all with this starting.
DOCTOR Go to, go to! You have known what you should not.
GENTLEWOMAN She has spoke what she should not, I am sure of
    that. Heaven knows what she has known. 40
LADY MACBETH Here's the smell of blood still. All the perfumes
    of Arabia will not sweeten this little hand. Oh, oh, oh!
DOCTOR What a sigh is there! The heart is sorely charged.
GENTLEWOMAN I would not have such a heart in my bosom for
    the dignity of the whole body. 45
DOCTOR Well, well, well.
GENTLEWOMAN Pray God it be, sir.
DOCTOR This disease is beyond my practice. Yet I have known those
    which have walked in their sleep who have died holily in their beds.
LADY MACBETH Wash your hands, put on your nightgown, look not so 50
    pale! I tell you yet again, Banquo's buried. He cannot come out
    on's grave.

GENTLEWOMAN It is customary for her, to seem to wash her hands.

    I've seen her do this for a quarter of an hour.   25

LADY MACBETH There's a spot here.

DOCTOR Listen, she speaks! I'll write down what she says to make sure

    I remember it correctly.

LADY MACBETH Out, damned spot! Out, I say! One; two. Why, then

    it's time to do it. Hell is murky. Shame, my lord, shame! A soldier,   30

    and afraid? Why should we fear who knows it, when none can

    challenge our account? Yet who would have thought the old

    man to have had so much blood in him?

DOCTOR Did you hear that?

LADY MACBETH The Thane of Fife had a wife. Where is she now?   35

    What, will these hands never be clean? No more of that, my lord,

    no more of that. You spoil everything with these sudden fits.

DOCTOR Shame, shame! You should not know such things.

GENTLEWOMAN She has said things she should not, I am sure of

    that. Heaven knows how she knows these things.   40

LADY MACBETH Here's still the smell of blood. All the perfumes

    of Arabia will not sweeten this little hand. Oh, oh, oh!

DOCTOR What a sigh! Her heart is heavy.

GENTLEWOMAN I would not have such a heart in my bosom, even

    to be a queen.   45

DOCTOR Well, well, well.

GENTLEWOMAN Pray God it be well, sir.

DOCTOR This disease is beyond my skills. Yet I have known those who

    have walked in their sleep and have died sinless in their beds.

LADY MACBETH Wash your hands, put on your nightgown, don't look   50

    so pale. I tell you yet again, Banquo's buried. He cannot come out

    of his grave.

DOCTOR Even so?

LADY MACBETH To bed, to bed! There's knocking at the gate.

> Come, come, come, come, give me your hand! What's done   55
>
> cannot be undone. To bed, to bed, to bed.

Exit LADY MACBETH

DOCTOR Will she go now to bed?

GENTLEWOMAN Directly.

DOCTOR Foul whisperings are abroad. Unnatural deeds

> Do breed unnatural troubles. Infected minds   60
>
> To their deaf pillows will discharge their secrets.
>
> More needs she the divine than the physician.
>
> God, God forgive us all! Look after her;
>
> Remove from her the means of all annoyance,
>
> And still keep eyes upon her. So good night.   65
>
> My mind she has mated, and amazed my sight.
>
> I think, but dare not speak.

GENTLEWOMAN Good night, good doctor.

Exeunt

Scene 2 [*The countryside, near Dunsiane*]

Drums and colors. Enter MENTEITH, CAITHNESS, ANGUS,
        LENNOX, SOLDIERS

MENTEITH The English Power is near, led on by Malcolm,

> His uncle Siward, and the good Macduff.
>
> Revenges burn in them; for their dear causes
>
> Would do the bleeding and the grim alarm
>
> Excite the mortified man.   5

ANGUS Near Birnam Wood

> Shall we well meet them; that way are they coming.

DOCTOR Even so?

LADY MACBETH To bed, to bed. There's knocking at the gate. Come,
come, come, come, give me your hand. What's done cannot be   55
undone. To bed, to bed, to bed.

Exit LADY MACBETH

DOCTOR Will she go to bed now?

GENTLEWOMAN Directly.

DOCTOR Rumors of evil deeds circulate. Unnatural deeds
Do breed unnatural troubles. Guilty minds   60
To their deaf pillows will whisper their secrets.
She has more need of the divine than the physician.
God, God forgive us all! Look after her;
Remove all means she has of harming herself,
And continually watch her. So, good night.   65
She has stunned my mind and amazed my sight.
I think, but dare not speak.

GENTLEWOMAN Good night, good doctor.

They exit

Scene 2 [*The countryside, near Dunsinane*]

Drums sound and military banners pass. Enter MENTEITH, CAITHNESS,
ANGUS, LENNOX, SOLDIERS

MENTEITH The English forces approach, led on by Malcolm,
His uncle Siward, and the good Macduff.
Revenge burns in them, for their heartfelt cause
Would excite even a dead man
To the bloody and grim call to arms.   5

ANGUS Near Birnam Wood
We'll likely meet them; they are coming that way.

CAITHNESS Who knows if Donalbain be with his brother?

LENNOX For certain, sir, he is not. I have a file

 Of all the gentry. There is Siward's son   10

 And many unrough youths that even now

 Protest their first manhood.

MENTEITH What does the tyrant?

CAITHNESS Great Dunsinane he strongly fortifies.

 Some say he's mad; others, that lesser hate him,   15

 Do call it valiant fury; but for certain

 He cannot buckle his distempered cause

 With the belt of rule.

ANGUS Now does he feel

 His secret murders sticking on his hands.   20

 Now minutely revolts upbraid his faith-breach.

 Those he commands move only in command,

 Nothing in love. Now does he feel his title

 Hang loose about him, like a giant's robe

 Upon a dwarfish thief.   25

MENTEITH Who then shall blame

 His pestered senses to recoil and start,

 When all that is within him does condemn

 Itself for being there?

CAITHNESS Well, march we on   30

 To give obedience where 'tis truly owed.

 Meet we the medicine of the sickly weal;

 And with him pour we in our country's purge

 Each drop of us.

CAITHNESS Who knows if Donalbain has joined his brother?

LENNOX For certain, sir, he has not. I have a list

    Of all the gentry. There is Siward's son,   10

    And many beardless youths that for the first time

    Declare they have reached manhood.

MENTEITH What is the tyrant doing?

CAITHNESS He strongly fortifies great Dunsinane.

    Some say he's mad; others, that hate him less,   15

    Do praise his valiant fury; but, for certain,

    He cannot buckle his swollen and diseased cause

    With the belt of self-control.

ANGUS Now does he feel

    His secret murders sticking on his hands;   20

    Every minute rebellions reproach his treachery.

    Those he commands move only because they're ordered,

    Not from love. Now does he feel his title

    Hang loose about him, like a giant's robe

    Upon a dwarfish thief.   25

MENTEITH Who then can wonder

    That his jangled nerves flinch in alarm;

    When he looks into his mind,

    His whole being condemns itself.

CAITHNESS Well, we must march on   30

    To do our duty where it's truly owed.

    We meet the physician for our sickly state,

    And with him, offer our blood,

    To help our country's cure.

LENNOX Or so much as it needs   35

    To dew the sovereign flower and drown the weeds.

    Make we our march towards Birnam.

Exeunt, marching

Scene 3 [*Dunsinane. A room in the castle*]

Enter MACBETH, DOCTOR, and ATTENDANTS

MACBETH Bring me no more reports. Let them fly all!

    Till Birnam Wood remove to Dunsinane,

    I cannot taint with fear. What's the boy Malcolm?

    Was he not born of woman? The spirits that know

    All mortal consequences have pronounced me thus: 5

    "Fear not, Macbeth. No man that's born of woman

    Shall e'er have power upon thee." Then fly, false thanes.

    And mingle with the English epicures.

    The mind I sway by and the heart I bear

    Shall never sag with doubt nor shake with fear.   10

Enter a SERVANT

    The devil damn thee black, thou cream-faced loon!

    Where got'st thou that goose look?

SERVANT There is ten thousand—

MACBETH Geese, villain?

SERVANT Soldiers, sir.   15

MACBETH Go prick they face and over-red thy fear.

    Thou lily-livered boy. What soldiers, patch?

    Death of thy soul! Those linen cheeks of thine

    Are counsellors to fear. What soldiers, wheyface?

SERVANT The English force, so please you.   20

LENNOX Or so much as it needs   35

    To water the sovereign flower and drown the weeds.

    Let's make our march toward Birnam.

                              Exit, marching

Scene 3 [*Dunsinane. A room in the castle*]

        Enter MACBETH, DOCTOR, *and* ATTENDANTS

MACBETH Bring me no more reports; send them all away.

    Till Birnam Wood shall move to Dunsinane,

    There's nothing for me to fear. Who's this boy Malcolm?

    Was he not born of woman? The spirits that know

    The outcome of all human affairs have said to me: 5

    "Fear not, Macbeth; no man that's born of woman

    Shall ever have power over you." So flee, false thanes,

    And mingle with the soft-living English.

    The mind that controls me and the heart I bear

    Shall never sag with doubt nor shake with fear.   10

               Enter a SERVANT

    The devil damn you black, you cream-faced loon!

    Where did you get that goose-like look?

SERVANT There are ten thousand—

MACBETH Geese, you slave?

SERVANT Soldiers, sir.   15

MACBETH Go cut your face, and cover your paleness with blood,

    You lily-livered boy. What soldiers, clown?

    Death to your soul! Those white cheeks of yours

    Persuade others to fear. What soldiers, cheese-face?

SERVANT The English troops, if it please you.   20

MACBETH Take thy face hence.

Exit SERVANT

Seyton!—I am sick at heart,

When I behold—Seyton, I say!—This push

Will cheer me ever, or disseat me now.

I have lived long enough. My way of life   25

Is fallen into the sere, the yellow leaf;

And that which should accompany old age,

As honor, love, obedience, troops of friends,

I must not look to have; but, in their stead,

Curses not loud but deep, mouth-honor, breath,   30

Which the poor heart would fain deny, and dare not.

Seyton!

Enter SEYTON

SEYTON What's your gracious pleasure?

MACBETH What news more?

SEYTON All is confirmed, my lord, which was reported.   35

MACBETH I'll fight, till from my bones my flesh be hacked.

Give me my armor.

SEYTON 'Tis not needed yet.

MACBETH I'll put it on.

Send out moe horses, skirr the country round;   40

Hang those that talk of fear. Give me mine armor.

How does your patient, doctor?

DOCTOR No so sick, my lord,

As she is troubled with thick-coming fancies

That keep her from her rest.   45

MACBETH Cure her of that!

Canst thou not minister to a mind diseased,

MACBETH Get your face out of here.

Exit SERVANT

    Seyton!—I am sick at heart

    When I behold—Seyton, I say!—This attack

    Will cheer me forever, or else dethrone me now.

    I have lived long enough. My way of life   25

    Has fallen into a withered state, a yellow leaf.

    And those things that should accompany old age,

    Such as honor, love, obedience, troops of friends,

    I must not seek to have; but, in their stead,

    Curses, whispered but deep, lip-service respect,   30

    Which the speaker would refuse if only he dared.

    Seyton!

Enter SEYTON

SEYTON What's your gracious pleasure?

MACBETH Is there any more news?

SEYTON All is confirmed, my lord, which was reported.   35

MACBETH I'll fight, till the flesh is hacked from my bones.

    Give me my armor.

SEYTON It's not needed yet.

MACBETH I'll put it on.

    Send out more horses, search the countryside;   40

    Hang those that talk of fear. Give me my armor.

    How is your patient, doctor?

DOCTOR Not as sick, my lord,

    As she's troubled with fantasies crowding upon each other

    That keep her from her rest.   45

MACBETH Then cure her of it!

    Can't you prescribe for a diseased mind,

Pluck from the memory a rooted sorrow,

Raze out the written troubles of the brain,

And with some sweet oblivious antidote   50

Cleanse the stuffed bosom of that perilous stuff

Which weighs upon the heart?

DOCTOR Therein the patient

Must minister to himself.

MACBETH Throw physic to the dogs, I'll none of it!   55

Come, put mine armor on. Give me my staff.

Seyton, send out.—Doctor, the thanes fly from me.—

Come, sir, dispatch. If thou couldst, doctor, cast

The water of my land, find her disease,

And purge it to a sound and pristine health,   60

I would applaud thee to the very echo,

That should applaud again.—Pull it off, I say.—

What rhubarb, senna, or what purgative drug,

Would scour these English hence? Hear'st thou of them?

DOCTOR Ay, my good lord. Your royal preparation   65

Makes us hear something.

MACBETH Bring it after me!

I will not be afraid of death and bane

Till Birnam Forest come to Dunsinane.

Exeunt all but the DOCTOR

DOCTOR Were I from Dunsinane away and clear,   70

Profit again should hardly draw me here.

Exit

Pluck from the memory a rooted sorrow,

Erase the troubles written on the brain,

And with some antidote of forgetfulness,   50

Cleanse the heavy heart of all the worries

That weigh upon it?

DOCTOR   In such cases the patient

Must cure himself.

MACBETH   Throw medicine to the dogs. I'll have none of it.   55

Come, put my armor on. Give me my lance.

Seyton, send out.—Doctor, the thanes desert me.—

Come, sir, hurry. If you could, doctor, examine

The urine of Scotland, find her disease,

And restore her to her sound and former healthy state,   60

I would applaud you until the very echo

Should applaud you again.— Pull it off, I say—

What rhubarb, senna, or other cleansing drug

Would scour these English away? Have you heard about them?

DOCTOR   Yes, my good lord. Your battle preparation   65

Makes us aware of their presence.

MACBETH   Bring my armor along.

I'll not fear death and pain

Till Birnam Forest comes to Dunsinane.

They all exit except the DOCTOR

DOCTOR   Had I left Dunsinane, free and clear,   70

No amount of profit would draw me here.

Exit DOCTOR

Scene 4 [*Countryside near Birnam Forest*]

Drums sound and military banners pass. Enter MALCOLM, SIWARD,

    MACDUFF, SIWARD'S SON, MENTEITH, CAITHNESS,

    ANGUS, LENNOX, ROSS, *and* SOLDIERS

MALCOLM Cousins, I hope the days are near at hand

    That chambers will be safe.

MENTEITH We doubt it nothing.

SIWARD What wood is this before us?

MENTEITH The Wood of Birnam.   5

MALCOLM Let every soldier hew him down a bough

    And bear't before him. Thereby shall we shadow

    The numbers of our host and make discovery

    Err in report of us.

SOLDIERS It shall be done.   10

SIWARD We learn no other but the confident tyrant

    Keeps still in Dunsinane and will endure

    Our setting down before't.

MALCOLM 'Tis his main hope;

    For where there is advantage to be given,   15

    Both more and less have given him the revolt;

    And none serve with him but constrained things,

    Whose hearts are absent too.

MACDUFF Let our just censures

    Attend the true event, and put we on   20

    Industrious soldiership.

SIWARD The time approaches

    That will with due decision make us know

    What we shall say we have, and what we owe.

    Thoughts speculative their unsure hopes relate,   25

Scene 4 [*Countryside near Birnam Forest*]

Drums sound and military banners pass. Enter MALCOLM, SIWARD,
      MACDUFF, SIWARD'S SON, MENTEITH, CAITHNESS,
      ANGUS, LENNOX, ROSS, *and* SOLDIERS

MALCOLM Comrades, I hope the day is near at hand
    When we can safely sleep in our beds.

MENTEITH We don't doubt that at all.

SIWARD What forest is this ahead?

MENTEITH Birnam Wood.   5

MALCOLM Let every soldier cut down a branch
    And hold it in front of him; that way we shall conceal
    The numbers of our force, and their scouts shall
    Error in their reports.

SOLDIERS It shall be done.   10

SIWARD Our reports show that the confident tyrant
    Is still in Dunsinane and hopes to
    Withstand our siege of it.

MALCOLM That's his best hope.
    For where there is a chance to escape,   15
    Those both high and low have rebelled against him.
    And none serve him but those who are compelled to,
    And their hearts are not in it.

MACDUFF Let us wait to judge
    Until we see the outcome, and till then,   20
    Concern ourselves with the fight.

SIWARD The time approaches
    That will surely show
    What we think we have and what we owe.
    Guesses only reflect our hopes;   25

But certain issue strokes must arbitrate;

Towards which advance the war.

Exeunt, marching

Scene 5 [*Dunsinane. Within the castle*]

            Enter MACBETH, SEYTON, *and* SOLDIERS

MACBETH Hang out our banners on the outward walls.

The cry is still, "They come!" Our castle's strength

Will laugh a siege to scorn. Here let them lie

Till famine and the ague eat them up.

Were they not forced with those that should be ours,   5

We might have met them dareful, beard to beard,

And beat them backward home.

A cry within of women.

What is that noise?

SEYTON It is the cry of women, my good lord.

He exits

MACBETH I have almost forgot the taste of fears.   10

The time has been, my senses would have cooled

To hear a night-shriek, and my fell of hair

Would at a dismal treatise rouse and stir

As life were in't. I have supped full with horrors.

Direness, familiar to my slaughterous thoughts,   15

Cannot once start me.

Enter SEYTON

Wherefore was that cry?

SEYTON The Queen, my lord, is dead.

Battle decides with surer strokes.

Let us get on with the war.

They exit marching

Scene 5 [*Dunsinane. Inside the castle*]

Enter MACBETH, SEYTON, *and* SOLDIERS

MACBETH Hang out our banners on the outer walls.

The cry is still, "They come!" Our castle's strength

Will laugh and scorn a siege. Here let them lie

Till famine and fever eat them up.

Were they not aided by deserters from our ranks,   5

We might have met them boldly, face to face,

And beat them backward home.

A cry of women offstage.

What is that noise?

SEYTON It is the cry of women, my good lord.

He exits

MACBETH I had almost forgotten the taste of fear.   10

The time once was when I would have been chilled

To hear a night-shriek, and the hair on my scalp

Would bristle at a grisly tale and rise

As though it were alive. Now I have supped full on horrors;

Horror, familiar to my slaughterous thoughts,   15

Cannot startle me.

Enter SEYTON

What was that cry?

SEYTON The Queen, my lord, is dead.

MACBETH She should have died hereafter;

    There would have been a time for such a word.   20

    Tomorrow, and tomorrow, and tomorrow

    Creeps in this petty pace from day to day

    To the last syllable of recorded time;

    And all our yesterdays have lighted fools

    The way to dusty death. Out, out, brief candle!   25

    Life's but a walking shadow, a poor player,

    That struts and frets his hour upon the stage

    And then is heard no more. It is a tale

    Told by an idiot, full of sound and fury,

    Signifying nothing.   30

Enter a MESSENGER

    Thou com'st to use thy tongue. Thy story quickly!

MESSENGER Gracious my lord,

    I should report that which I say I saw,

    But know not how to do't.

MACBETH Well, say, sir!   35

MESSENGER As I did stand my watch upon the hill,

    I looked toward Birnam, and anon methought

    The wood began to move.

MACBETH Liar and slave!

MESSENGER Let me endure your wrath if't be not so.   40

    Within this three mile may you see it coming;

    I say, a moving grove.

MACBETH If thou speak'st false,

    Upon the next tree shalt thou hang alive,

    Till famine cling thee. If thy speech be sooth,   45

MACBETH She had to die sometime.

    But I could have picked a better time for such news.   20

    Tomorrow, and tomorrow, and tomorrow

    Creeps in this petty pace from day to day

    To the last syllable of recorded time,

    And all our yesterdays have lighted fools

    The way to dusty death. Out, out, brief candle!   25

    Life's but a walking shadow, a poor player

    That struts and frets his hour upon the stage

    And then is heard no more. It is a tale

    Told by an idiot, full of sound and fury,

    Signifying nothing.   30

                    Enter a MESSENGER

    You're here to speak; tell your story quickly.

MESSENGER My gracious lord,

    I should report that which I say I saw,

    But know not how to do it.

MACBETH Well, say it, sir!   35

MESSENGER As I did stand my watch upon the hill,

    I looked toward Birnam, and soon I thought

    The wood began to move.

MACBETH Liar and slave!

MESSENGER May I suffer your wrath if it weren't so.   40

    Within three miles, you may see it coming;

    I mean, a moving forest.

MACBETH If you speak false,

    You shall hang alive upon the next tree

    Till famine shrivels you. If your speech is true,   45

I care not if thou dost for me as much.

I pull in resolution, and begin

To doubt the equivocation of the fiend

That lies like truth. "Fear not, till Birnam Wood

Do come to Dunsinane!" And now a wood   50

Comes toward Dunsinane. Arm, arm, and out!

If this which he avouches does appear,

There is not flying hence nor tarrying here.

I 'gin to be aweary of the sun,

And wish the estate of the world were now undone.   55

Ring the alarm bell! Blow wind, come wrack,

At least we'll die with harness on our back!

Exeunt

Scene 6 [*Dunsinane. Before the castle*]

Drum and Colors. Enter MALCOLM, SIWARD, MACDUFF, *and their*
army, carrying boughs

MALCOLM Now near enough. Your leafy screens throw down

And show like those you are. You,

worthy uncle,

Shall with my cousin, your right noble son,

Lead our first battle. Worthy Macduff and we   5

Shall take upon's what else remains to do,

According to our order.

SIWARD Fare you well.

Do we but find the tyrant's power tonight,

Let us be beaten if we cannot fight.   10

MACDUFF Make all our trumpets speak, give them all breath,

Those clamorous harbingers of blood and death.

Exeunt. Alarums continued

I care not if you do the same to me.

I tighten my resolution and begin

To suspect the two-faced promises of the fiend

That lies like truth: "Fear not, till Birnam Wood

Does come to Dunsinane!" And now a wood   50

Comes toward Dunsinane. To arms, to arms, and go!

If what he says is really true,

There's no security in flying or in staying here.

I begin to tire of the sun,

And wish the structure of the universe were undone.   55

Ring the alarm bell! Blow wind, come ruin!

At least we'll die with armor on our back.

They exit

Scene 6 [*The countryside, near Dunsinane*]

Drums sound and military banners pass. Enter MALCOLM, SIWARD,
     MACDUFF, *and their army, carrying boughs*

MALCOLM Now near enough. Throw away your leafy screens,

And show yourselves as the soldiers that you are. You,
          worthy uncle,

Shall with my cousin, your right noble son,

Lead our main force. Worthy Macduff and we   5

Shall take upon us what remains to do,

According to our plan of battle.

SIWARD Fare you well.

If we do find the tyrant's army tonight,

Let us be beaten if we do not fight.   10

MACDUFF Make all our trumpets speak; give them all breath,

Those noisy heralds of blood and death.

They exit, with trumpets sounding

171

Scene 7 [*Another part of the field*]

Enter MACBETH

MACBETH They have tied me to a stake. I cannot fly,
    But bear-like I must fight the course. What's he
    That was not born of woman? Such a one
    Am I to fear, or none.

Enter YOUNG SIWARD

YOUNG SIWARD What is thy name?   5

MACBETH Thou'lt be afraid to hear it.

YOUNG SIWARD No; though thou call'st thyself a hotter name
    Than any is in hell.

MACBETH My name's Macbeth.

YOUNG SIWARD The devil himself could not pronounce a title   10
    More hateful to mine ear.

MACBETH No, nor more fearful.

YOUNG SIWARD Thou liest, abhorred tyrant! With my sword
    I'll prove the lie thou speak'st.

[*They fight, and* YOUNG SIWARD *is slain*]

MACBETH Thou wast born of woman.   15
    But swords I smile at, weapons laugh to scorn,
    Brandished by man that's of a woman born.

He exits

Alarums. Enter MACDUFF

MACDUFF That way the noise is. Tyrant, show thy face!
    If thou be'st slain and with no stroke of mine,
    My wife and children's ghosts will haunt me still.   20
    I cannot strike at wretched kerns, whose arms
    Are hired to bear their staves. Either thou, Macbeth,

Scene 7 [*Another part of the field*]

Enter MACBETH

MACBETH They have tied me to a stake. I cannot escape,
  But like a baited bear, I must fight the course. Who's this man
  That was not from woman born? Such a one
  Am I to fear, or none at all.

Enter YOUNG SIWARD

YOUNG SIWARD What is your name?   5

MACBETH You would be afraid to hear it.

YOUNG SIWARD No, though you'd call yourself by a hotter name
  Than any there's in hell.

MACBETH My name's Macbeth.

YOUNG SIWARD The devil himself could not pronounce a name   10
  More hateful to my ear.

MACBETH No, nor more fearful.

YOUNG SIWARD You lie, hated tyrant, and with my sword
  I'll prove your lie.

[*They fight, and* YOUNG SIWARD *is slain*]

MACBETH You were born of woman.   15
  But swords I smile at and weapons laugh to scorn
  Brandished by a man that's of a woman born.

He exits

Trumpets sound. Enter MACDUFF

MACDUFF The noise comes from there. Tyrant, show your face.
  If you are slain by any stroke but mine,
  My wife and children's ghosts will haunt me forever.   20
  I shall not strike at wretched soldiers, whose arms
  Were bought to bear their spears. Either you, Macbeth,

Or else my sword with an unbattered edge

I sheathe again undeeded. There thou shouldst be.

By this great clatter one of greatest note 25

Seems bruited. Let me find him, Fortune!

And more I beg not.

He exits

Alarum. Enter MALCOLM *and* SIWARD

SIWARD This way, my lord. The castle's gently rendered:

The tyrant's people on both sides do fight;

The noble thanes do bravely in the war; 30

The day almost itself professes yours,

And little is to do.

MALCOLM We have met with foes

That strike beside us.

SIWARD Enter, sir, the castle. 35

Alarum.

They exit

Scene 8 [*Another part of the field*]

Enter MACBETH

MACBETH Why should I play the Roman fool and die

On mine own sword? Whiles I see lives, the gashes

Do better upon them.

Enter MACDUFF

MACDUFF Turn, hellhound, turn!

MACBETH Of all men else I have avoided thee. 5

But get thee back! My soul is too much charged

With blood of thine already.

Or else my sword with an unbattered edge

I sheath again unused. You must be over there;

All this racket seems to proclaim   25

One of your renown. Let me find him, Fortune!

And more I will not ask.

Trumpets sound.

                             Exit MACDUFF

           Enter MALCOLM *and* SIWARD

SIWARD This way, my lord. The castle has peacefully surrendered.

The tyrant's people on both sides do help;

The noble thanes do bravely in the war;   30

The day almost announces itself as yours,

And little's left to do.

MALCOLM We have met with foes

That deliberately miss us with their blows.

SIWARD Enter, sir, the castle.   35

Trumpets sound.

                            They exit

Scene 8 [*Another part of the field*]

             Enter MACBETH

MACBETH Why should I play the Roman fool and die

On my own sword? While I see living enemies, I'll still

Try to fight.

             Enter MACDUFF

MACDUFF Turn, hellhound, turn!

MACBETH You, of all men, I have avoided.   5

But now get back! My soul is too much burdened

With the blood of your line already.

MACDUFF I have no words;

My voice is in my sword, thou bloodier villain

Than terms can give thee out!   10

Alarum. They fight

MACBETH Thou losest labor.

As easy mayst thou the intrenchant air

With they keen sword impress as make me bleed.

Let fall they blade on vulnerable crests.

I bear a charmed life, which must not yield   15

To one of woman born.

MACDUFF Despair they charm!

And let the angel whom thou still hast served

Tell thee, Macduff was from his mother's womb

Untimely ripped.   20

MACBETH Accursed be that tongue that tells me so,

For it hath cowed my better part of man!

And be these juggling fiends no more believed,

That palter with us in a double sense,

That keep the word of promise to our ear   25

And break it to our hope! I'll not fight with thee!

MACDUFF Then yield thee, coward,

And live to be the show and gaze o' the time!

We'll have, as our rarer monsters are,

Painted upon a pole, and underwrit   30

"Here may you see the tyrant."

MACBETH I will not yield,

To kiss the ground before young Malcolm's feet

And to be baited with the rabble's curse.

Though Birnam Wood be come to Dunsinane,   35

MACDUFF I have no words.

    My voice is my sword, you villain bloodier

    Than words can describe!   10

Trumpet sounds. They fight

MACBETH You waste your energy.

    You can as easily cut the invulnerable air

    With your keen sword as make me bleed.

    Let your blade fall on vulnerable heads;

    I bear a charmed life, which is fated not to yield   15

    To one of woman born.

MACDUFF Forget your charm,

    And let the evil angel whom you have served

    Tell you, Macduff was from his mother's womb

    Untimely ripped, not born.   20

MACBETH Accursed be the tongue that tells me so,

    For it has destroyed all my resolve.

    And let no one believe those deceiving fiends,

    They trifle with us in words of double meanings;

    So they may keep their promise to our ear,   25

    And break it to our hope. I'll not fight with you.

MACDUFF Then yield, you coward,

    And live to be the spectacle of the age.

    We'll display you, as rare freaks are,

    Your picture painted and hung on a pole,   30

    And underneath, "Here you may see the tyrant."

MACBETH I will not yield

    To kiss the ground before young Malcolm's feet

    And be baited by the rabble's curse.

    Though Birnam Wood did come to Dunsinane   35

And thou opposed, being of no woman born,

Yet I will try the last. Before my body

I throw my warlike shield. Lay on, Macduff,

And damned be him that first cries, "Hold, enough!"

Alarums. Exeunt fighting

Retreat and flourish. Drum and colors.

       Enter MALCOLM, SIWARD, ROSS, THANES, *and* SOLDIERS

MALCOLM I would the friends we miss were safe arrived.

SIWARD Some must go off; and yet, by these I see,

    So great a day as this is cheaply bought.

MALCOLM Macduff is missing, and your noble son.

ROSS Your son, my lord, has paid a soldier's debt.   5

    He only lived but till he was a man.

    The which no sooner had his prowess confirmed

    In the unshrinking station where he fought

    But like a man he died.

SIWARD Then he is dead?   10

ROSS Ay, and brought off the field. Your cause of sorrow

    Must not be measured by his worth, for then

    It hath no end.

SIWARD Had he his hurts before?

ROSS Ay, on the front.   15

SIWARD Why then, God's soldier be he!

    Had I as many sons as I have hairs,

    I would not wish them to a fairer death.

    And so his knell is knolled.

MALCOLM He's worth more sorrow,   20

    And that I'll spend for him.

SIWARD He's worth no more.

And you oppose me and are not of woman born,

Yet I will fight to the end. I throw down

My warrior's shield. Lay on, Macduff,

And damned be him that first cries, "Hold, enough!"

Trumpet sounds. They exit fighting

Trumpet sounds. Drums sound and military banners pass.

   Enter MALCOLM, SIWARD, ROSS, THANES, *and* SOLDIERS

MALCOLM I wish the friends we miss were safely here.

SIWARD Some must die; and yet, judging by what I see,

 So great a day as this was cheaply bought.

MALCOLM Macduff is missing, and your noble son.

ROSS Your son, my lord, has paid a soldier's debt.   5

 He only lived until he was a man,

 And no sooner had his valor confirmed this

 In the post from which he fought without flinching,

 Than like a man he died.

SIWARD Then he is dead?   10

ROSS Yes, and brought off the field. Your cause of sorrow

 Must not be measured by his worth, for then

 It has no end.

SIWARD His wounds were on the front?

ROSS Yes, on the front.   15

SIWARD Why then, God's soldier he is.

 Had I as many sons as I have hairs,

 I would not wish them to a fairer death.

 Let the funeral bells be tolled.

MALCOLM He's worth more sorrow,   20

 And that I'll spend for him.

SIWARD He's worth no more.

They say he parted well and paid his score,

And so, God be with him! Here comes newer comfort.

Enter MACDUFF with MACBETH'S head

MACDUFF Hail, King! for so thou art. Behold where stands   25

    The usurper's cursed head. The time is free.

    I see thee compassed with thy kingdom's pearl,

    That speak my salutation in their minds;

    Whose voices I desire aloud with mine—

    Hail, King of Scotland!   30

ALL Hail, King of Scotland!

Flourish.

MALCOLM We shall not spend a large expense of time

    Before we reckon with your several loves

    And make us even with you. My thanes and kinsmen,

    Henceforth be Earls, the first that ever Scotland   35

    In such an honor named. What's more to do

    Which should be planted newly with the time—

    As calling home our exiled friends abroad

    That fled the snares of watchful tyranny,

    Producing forth the cruel ministers   40

    Of this dead butcher and his fiendlike queen,

    Who, as 'tis thought, by self and violent hands

    Took off her life—this, and what needful else

    That calls upon us, by the grace of Grace

    We will perform in measure, time, and place.   45

    So thanks to all at once, and to each one.

    Whom we invite to see us crowned as Scone.

Flourish.

Exeunt omnes

They say he died well and paid his debts;

And so God be with him. Here comes newer comfort.

Enter MACDUFF *with* MACBETH'S *head*

MACDUFF Hail, King! for so you are. Behold, where stands   25

The usurper's cursed head. Our country's free.

I see you surrounded with your kingdom's best,

That echo my greeting in their hearts,

And whose voices I want to hear with mine:

Hail, King of Scotland!   30

ALL Hail, King of Scotland!

Trumpet sounds.

MALCOLM We shall not waste a great deal of time

Before we reward the love that each of you has shown,

And pay our debts to you. My thanes and kinsmen,

Now be called "earls," the first that ever Scotland   35

In such an honor named. There's more to do,

Which should be done afresh with this new era,

Such as calling home our exiled friends abroad

That fled the snares of suspicious tyranny,

Seeking out the cruel agents   40

Of this dead butcher and his fiend-like queen,

Who, as it was thought, by her own violent hands

Took her own life—this, and anything else

That demands our attention, by the grace of God,

We will perform in due order, time, and place.   45

So thanks to all at once, and to each one,

Whom we invite to see us crowned at Scone.

Trumpet sounds.

All exit

Glossary

The following terms are taken from the translation of *The Tragedy of Macbeth*. The scene and line numbers are given in parentheses after the terms, which are listed in the order they first occur.

Act One

hurlyburly (scene 1, line 3): uproar, tumult—of the battle described in the next scene

gray cat, demon toad (scene 1, lines 9-10): spirits embodied in animals that attend and serve a person

Forres (scene 2, stage direction): site of the royal palace of Duncan, 11 miles southwest of Elgin, Scotland

Western Isles (scene 2, line 14): Ireland and the Hebrides, off the western coast of Scotland

Golgotha (scene 2, line 43): "place of the skull," where Christ was crucified

thane (scene 2, line 49): a title of Scottish nobility, roughly that of an earl in England

Fife (scene 2, line 54): area in eastern Scotland; site of Macduff's castle

Saint Colme's Isle (scene 2, line 69): an island in the Firth of Forth, a tidal mouth on the eastern coast of Scotland

Aleppo (scene 3, line 7): city in northern Syria

Weird Sisters (scene 3, line 32): sisters of fate or destiny; the three witches

blasted heath (scene 3, line 78): a flat, bare tract of wasteland, withered by storms and lightning

Inverness (scene 4, line 48): site of Macbeth's castle in northwest Scotland

Act Two

Hecate (scene 1, line 60): goddess of witchcraft and magic

Tarquin (scene 1, line 63): Sixth-century Roman tyrant

bellman (scene 2, line 3): town crier who tolled a bell on the night before an execution

183

Neptune   (scene 2, line 72): the Roman god of the sea

incarnadine   (scene 2, line 74): blood red

Beelzebub   (scene 3, line 3): one of the chief devils

Gorgon   (scene 3, line 74): a mythological creature whose glance turned people to stone

Scone   (scene 4, line 39): the ancient capital of Scotland

Colmekill   (scene 4, line 42): small island, now called Iona, where Scottish kings were buried

Act Three

parricide   (scene 1, line 35): the killing of a parent

Mark Antony   (scene 1, line 61): according to the Greek biographer Plutarch, Mark Antony was told by a fortune teller that his future would be darkened so long as he remained in the company of Octavius Caesar

curfew bell   (scene 2, line 48): a bell sounded at evening

Hyrcan tiger   (scene 4, line 118): a tiger from the ancient region of Hyricania, south of the Caspian Sea

Acheron   (scene 5, line 15): in Greek mythology, a river in the underworld.

Act Four

adder's fork   (scene 1, line 16): the forked tongue of a snake

slowworm   (scene 1, line 16): a small limbless lizard.

Birnam Wood   (scene 1, line 102): a wooded hill about 12 miles from Dunsinane Castle in Scotland

twofold orbs and triple scepters   (scene 1, line 132): symbols of sovereignty; the orbs refer to England and Scotland; the scepters, to England, Scotland, and Ireland

lime   (scene 2, line 39): a sticky substance smeared on branches to catch birds

Lucifer   (scene 3, line 26): Satan's name before his fall

the Evil   (scene 3, line 165): scrofula; tuberculoses of the lymph nodes in the neck; it was believed that the king's touch could cure this disease

fell   (scene 3, line 257): fierce

Act Five

baited bear   (scene 7, line 2): in Elizabethan times, bears were chained to posts and attacked by dogs for sport

Roman fool   (scene 8, line 1): commit suicide; Roman officers considered it honorable to kill themselves to avoid capture when defeated

Untimely ripped   (scene 8, line 20): prematurely delivered, by a Caesarean section operation